CASINO GAMES

by
BILL FRIEDMAN

Photography: Len Jossel

Under the general editorship of
VERA R. WEBSTER

GOLDEN PRESS • NEW YORK
WESTERN PUBLISHING COMPANY, INC.
RACINE, WISCONSIN

FOREWORD

CASINO GAMES is a guide to the five most popular games usually offered by casinos—Twenty-One, Craps, Keno, Baccarat, and Roulette. They appear in the order of their popularity and the text describes every bet currently offered by Nevada casinos as well as many variations found in casinos in the rest of the world. Full color photographs and illustrations complement the text so that the reader can see the actual operation of the games. This guide is designed to inform the reader of every bet, explaining each in detail: describing the location where each wager is made, the proper procedure for making each wager, the way the dealers will handle each wager if they are required to move it, the customary way in which dealers pay off each wager when it wins, and the location where each payoff is made.

The author would like to extend his appreciation to those who have contributed, in a special way to the development of this book, particularly to E. J. Legere and Harley Kaufman for reading critically the chapters on Keno and Baccarat respectively; to Mark Swain, who introduced the author to the general editor and made possible this publication; to Cecil E. Jones for his editorial assistance; and to the world champion poker player, "Amarillo Slim" Preston, who appears in the photograph (p. 8) of the Twenty-One game being played at Binion's Horseshoe Club in downtown Las Vegas.

WDF

Photo Credits: All photographs in this book were taken by Leonard Jossel at The Las Vegas Hilton, Binion's Horseshoe Club, and the Stardust Hotel.

TABLE OF CONTENTS

INTRODUCTION

Recreation plays a very important role in the lives of most people and casino games may be considered as one form of recreation, the object being to win, to stretch one's recreation dollar to gain a maximum of playing pleasure, or to play for the sheer enjoyment of matching wits with the laws of probabilities. This guide is designed to teach the beginner the rules of the games, eliminating the beginner's reluctance to expose his ignorance of the game, and to explain all bets in such a way that any player may develop his proficiency to add enjoyment to playing the game as well as extending the use of his recreation funds. It is also a valuable reference work for the experienced casino customer since it explains the mathematical principles of each game, which the novice can quickly skim. Gambling may be considered a "love affair with chance," but no one should gamble with money he cannot afford to lose.

This guide presents the most commonly used gambling terms in each bet description, and each term is defined the first time it is used. This increases the reader's knowledge and will make him more comfortable when he enters a casino setting. The layouts, with slight variations, are basic to all casinos, but the illustrations in this book are patterned after the layouts used by the Las Vegas Hilton. Where a comparison is relevant, the Crap illustrations are designed like the layouts used by Harrah's at Reno and Lake Tahoe.

Most importantly, this guide reveals the best bets, the ones having the lowest casino advantage, offered by each game; and it explains the reasons mathematically. The casino advantage percentage, which creates the casino's profit, is listed for every bet so the reader can compare the relative merits of each game and the bets it offers. The meaning of casino advantage is explained on pages 6 and 7.

A customer can wager either money or chips at any of the table games, but the dealer always pays off winning wagers with chips in denominations of $1, $5, $25, $100, $500, and sometimes in denominations of 25¢ and 50¢. This guide describes the correct method used by a customer to buy chips at each of the games. When a customer concludes his playing, hopefully a winner, he takes his chips to the casino cashier's cage, prominantly located in the casino, and exchanges the chips for U.S. currency.

Almost all casinos give complimentary cocktails to customers as they play, and these drinks are served on the edge of the tables in front of the customers playing Twenty-One, Roulette, and Baccarat. At a Crap table, drinks are served on a shelf that runs around it, and ladies can place their handbags on this shelf.

Many customers tip dealers, but this custom is completely optional. There are no established standards, so each customer should use his own judgment and tip according to his own value system. Some customers make an occasional small wager for the dealer, which the dealer collects if the bets win (customers should always inform the dealer when wagers are made for him); other customers tip occasionally either while playing or when they leave the table. A gratuity is in order if a dealer is particularly helpful. On the other hand, if a dealer is rude or refuses to explain the casino's rules, the customer should either move to another table, or go to another casino where he feels more comfortable and is treated more courteously.

CASINO ADVANTAGE

A casino earns its profits by charging its customers a fee for the privilege of participating in each gambling transaction. This fee is called the "casino advantage," which is an average percentage the casino takes out of each wager; it is illustrated in the following coin flipping example:

If a customer were to flip a coin against a hypothetical casino and wager $1 that every flip would be heads, he would lose $1 on every flip that tails appeared. However, the casino would only pay 99¢ when the customer flipped a head and won, so the customer would only win an average of 99¢ for every $1 he lost. The customer would be out 1¢ for every two flips he wagered; therefore, he could expect to lose 1¢ for every $2 invested. One cent is .5 percent (the casino advantage) of $2.

A casino expects to win the casino advantage percentage of a customer's total "wagering handle," which is the value of all his wagers added together. For example, a customer who buys $100 in chips and wagers one $1 chip at a time may actually make thousands of dollars worth of wagers; and if the casino advantage in this example is 1 percent, the customer will make an average of 10,000 wagers before he loses his $100 bankroll, because 1 percent of a wagering handle of $10,000 equals the $100 bankroll.

Even though a casino customer experiences only a small finite number of decisions, it is realistic to assume he will encounter a normal sample of the statistical distribution because most customers do; and large casinos generate so much business, they almost always win the expected casino advantage percentage from their customers' total wagering handle each year.

As a customer continues to make more wagers, he increases the probability he will lose an amount equal to the casino advantage percentage, because as he makes more wagers, he decreases the likelihood he will experience a deviant sample. Also, as a customer increases his wagering, he must expect to lose a greater amount, because the casino expects to win a certain percentage of his total wagering handle. When these two statistical principles are compounded, it becomes clear that a customer who wants to maximize his probability of winning should make as few wagers as possible. Ideally, a customer should take all the money he intends to gamble during his lifetime and wager it at one time on the bet with the lowest casino advantage.

Many customers use the following three types of systems in a vain attempt to alter the casino advantage, but these systems have no long run effect.

(1) Some customers utilize "money management." They vary the size of their wager according to whether they won or lost the last wager, but this has no long term statistical effect. For example, a customer can vary the size of his wagers to increase the likelihood of winning, but this results in a corresponding decrease in the amount he can expect to win.

(2) Some customers do not understand the "law of averages." For instance, 12 will appear on an average of once in every 36 rolls of the dice, so some customers do not wager until 12 has not appeared for 100 rolls, incorrectly assuming that 12 is more likely to appear. The dice have no memory.

(3) Some customers attempt to protect their money by combining several wagers on the same layout in such a way that when one loses, another wins, etc., but the casino advantage remains the same for every individual bet no matter what combination of wagers is made.

7

In the game Twenty-One, both the player and dealer attempt to get as close to a card count of 21 as possible without exceeding it. It is the only casino game in which the customer is not permitted to wager on every possible alternative. Specifically, he is not allowed to wager on the dealer's hand or the other customers' hands. He should only be concerned with the relationship of his own hand with the dealer's hand, since the actions of the other players will not have an appreciable long-term effect on whether he wins or loses.

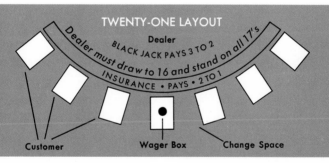

TWENTY-ONE LAYOUT

Dealer

BLACK JACK PAYS 3 TO 2

Dealer must draw to 16 and stand on all 17's

INSURANCE • PAYS • 2 TO 1

Customer   Wager Box   Change Space

TO MAKE A WAGER, either chips or currency may be used. Each player should place the amount of his wager in the box directly in front of his chair. Wagers can be made at any time before the cards are dealt, but the wager should never be touched after the first card is received. When a player wagers a greater amount of currency than the table minimum in a betting box, the dealer will usually ask, "change or play?" When a player wants his currency changed into chips or wants his chips converted into another denomination, he should place them between boxes to signify "change" or "no bet"; everything placed in a box represents a wager. While a hand is in progress, the dealer cannot make change. At the conclusion of the hand the dealer will place change in front of player.

MINIMUM AND MAXIMUM WAGERS are prominently displayed at each table along with other playing rules. The minimum wager is generally $1.00 although a few casinos still have a $.50 minimum. Major casinos often have some tables with a $5.00 minimum. Larger wagers are permitted in increments of $.50 ($1.50, $2.00, $2.50, etc.). The traditional maximum wager is $500, but each casino sets its own limits. In any event, the player should be aware of the minimum and maximum wagers before play begins.

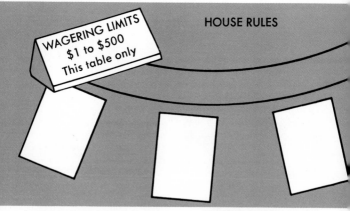

HOUSE RULES

WAGERING LIMITS
$1 to $500
This table only

CARD SUITS—Spades, Hearts, Diamonds and Clubs—have no significance and are disregarded. The point value of the cards determines the outcome of the game. Two through 9 equal face value, as shown. Tens, Jacks, Queens and Kings have a value of 10. Aces count either 1 or 11 at the player's option. The customer should always count an ace as 11 unless the value of the total hand would be more than 21.

CARD VALUES

EACH CARD = FACE VALUE

EACH CARD = 10 POINTS

AN ACE = 1 OR 11

Single Deck

4-Deck Shoe

THE GAME IS PLAYED with either one standard 52-card deck or with four standard decks, which are dealt from a dealing device called a "shoe." Both dealing styles have the same rules.

THE CUT is offered by the dealer to the player of his choice after the cards have been shuffled. Each player may refuse to cut, but if they all do, then the dealer must make the cut himself. The player should use only one hand to make a single cut towards the middle of the deck. The dealer will complete the cut. In multi-deck games, and many single deck games, the dealer retains possession of the shuffled deck, and the player cuts the deck with a joker.

Cutting a Single Deck

Cutting a Multiple Deck

The Burn Card

THE "BURN" CARD is the first card the dealer removes from the deck. He places it face up at the bottom of the deck, or face down in the discard tray. All cards used in a hand are discarded in the same way. The first and last cards are never used in a hand, even when the dealer runs out of cards during the play of a hand. When the dealer runs out of cards during a hand, he must shuffle and continue dealing at the position of interruption. The casino may allow the dealer to shuffle at any point in the game unless a hand is in progress.

Alternative method of "burning"

THE DEAL begins when all the players have made their wagers. The dealer begins with the player to the right at First Base and deals in a clockwise order. He deals one card to each player and one face-up card to himself. He deals a second card to each player and slides a "Hole" card face down under his initial face-up card. The player immediately picks up his two cards and determines the total. He should hold the two cards completely off the table in only one hand to avoid bending them or removing them from the dealer's sight.

THE DEAL

Third Base

First Base

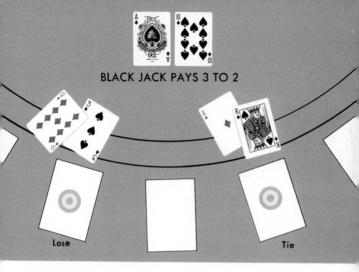

BLACK JACK PAYS 3 TO 2

BLACKJACK occurs when the dealer's first two cards (an Ace with any 10-value card) total 21. If the dealer's face-up card is either an Ace or a 10-value card, he must look at his face-down card to determine if he has Blackjack. When the dealer has Blackjack he turns up his Hole card and terminates the hand. All players lose except those who also have Blackjack which is a tie (also called a "push" or "standoff") and means the player's wager is neither won nor lost.

When a player has Blackjack he immediately lays his two cards face up in front of his wager. He wins and receives a payoff of 3 to 2 unless the dealer also has Blackjack. All other bets, except Insurance which is explained later, are paid 1 to 1. Many years ago, Nevada casinos occasionally offered special bonus payments for certain hands, but this policy has been in disuse.

A PLAYER "STANDS" (asks for no more cards) when he is satisfied with his hand. The player indicates that he stands by sliding his original two cards under his wager, which should then not be touched. In clockwise rotation the dealer completes each player's hand beginning with First Base, the player on the right of the table. The dealer only stops at each player who is still holding his original two cards.

A "HIT" (an additional card) is requested by the player when he wants to increase his total point count. The player can obtain an additional card by brushing the edge of his original two cards over the table, or by making a beckoning motion with his hand. The dealer will then place another card face up in front of the player and next to his original cards. After each "hit," the player may continue to draw as many cards as he wishes unless his total count exceeds 21.

THE PLAYER "BREAKS" (loses) if he hits and his card total goes over 21. He immediately turns his original two cards face up and lays them on the dealer's side of his wager. The dealer takes the player's cards and the losing wager and places the cards in the discard tray. Then, the dealer goes to the next player and continues to deal in a clockwise direction around the table until all players have had a chance to complete their hands.

Face-up dealing

FACE UP DEALING is practiced at many casinos. When the player's original two cards are dealt face up, he does not handle them. He obtains a "hit" by scratching one or more fingers towards himself next to his cards and "stands" by holding his open palm up to the dealer, who then proceeds to the next hand. It is better for a beginning player to play at a table where the cards are dealt face up because it is easier to ask the dealer for advice when the dealer can see the cards. The dealer must play by fixed rules so his actions are not influenced if the player's cards are exposed.

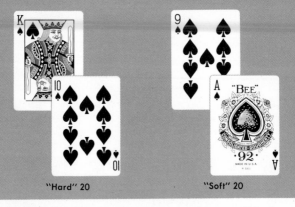

"Hard" 20   "Soft" 20

A HARD HAND either contains no Aces, or if it does, each Ace is counted as 1.

A SOFT HAND contains one or more Aces in which one Ace can be counted as 11 and the total count of the hand will not exceed 21. The player should always count an Ace as 11 until his count exceeds 21. He then subtracts 10 from his total which makes the Ace count only 1.

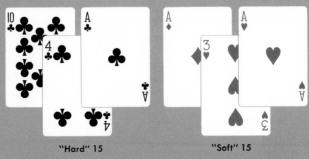

"Hard" 15   "Soft" 15

18

FIXED RULES are featured at most casinos. When all players' hands have been completed, the dealer turns up his Hole card and plays out his hand according to fixed rules. The dealer must always hit a Hard 16 or less and stand on Hard 17 or more. All casinos stand on Soft 18 or more, but the Las Vegas Strip also stands on Soft 17, a slight advantage to the player. If the dealer goes over 21, he breaks and must pay off all wagers. Any player who has gone over 21 has already lost his wager.

DEALER'S HITTING RULE
(Dealer must draw to 16 or under)

Lose

Lose

Tie

Win

A CUSTOMER WINS if he has a total card count higher than the dealer's final count but not over 21. When the dealer stands with a count of 17 to 21, he pays off all players who have a card count higher than his and collects from those with a lesser total. When both dealer and player stand with the same total between 17 and 21, no money changes hands. The dealer indicates the tie and removes the player's cards without touching the wager. After a player wins, or ties, his money remains for the next hand unless he alters his wager or quits playing.

THE BASIC STRATEGY for playing Twenty-One has been determined by several computer experts, and it is the correct strategy to play for the first deal of a newly shuffled deck or from a deck in which unknown cards have already been played out and discarded. The principle of basic strategy is to balance the probability of the player going broke against the probability of the dealer having a "Pat" hand (a total count of 17, 18, 19, 20, or 21).

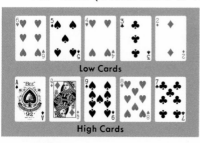

Low Cards

High Cards

The player's decision is based on the point count of the dealer's face-up card, which determines the probabilities of each type of point count he can achieve.

A STIFF is a card count of Hard 12 to Hard 16. The player should always draw to a Hard total of less than 12 because his total count can increase without the possibility of his going over 21. He should always stand with a Hard total of more than 16 because he has a "Pat" hand (a count of 17 to 21). The only totals the player should hit that might cause him to go over 21 are Hard 12 to Hard 16. The player must decide whether to hit or stand.

IN HARD HAND HITTING STRATEGY, the player should hit all Stiffs even though he risks "breaking," if the dealer has a high face-up card of 7 to Ace. With a high face-up card, the dealer has a high probability of achieving a "Pat" hand (17 to 21). If the dealer has a low face-up card of 2 to 6, he must hit to obtain the required minimum of 17 and risk "breaking," except in casinos where the dealer stands on Soft 17. The dealer does not hit a 6 with an Ace in the hole.

HARD HAND HITTING STRATEGY

PLAYER	DEALER'S CARD									
	2	3	4	5	6	7	8	9	10	A
17										
16						Hit	Hit	Hit	Hit	Hit
15						Hit	Hit	Hit	Hit	Hit
14						Hit	Hit	Hit	Hit	Hit
13						Hit	Hit	Hit	Hit	Hit
12	Hit	Hit				Hit	Hit	Hit	Hit	Hit

☐ Stand

▨ Hit

When the dealer has a low face-up card, the player should not hit a Stiff and risk "breaking."

SOFT HAND HITTING STRATEGY indicates the player should always hit a soft hand of 17 or less because these counts only win when the dealer "breaks." The player risks giving up an occasional "push" when the dealer also has 17, but he improves his total much more often. The player should hit Soft 18 only if the dealer has a face-up card of 9 or 10. When the player hits and obtains a Soft total over 21, he subtracts 10 to make it a Hard total under 21.

The only exception is when he has a Hard 12 and the dealer's faceup card is a 2 or 3.

SOFT HAND HITTING STRATEGY

PLAYER	DEALER'S CARD									
	2	3	4	5	6	7	8	9	10	A
19										
18								Hit	Hit	
17	Hit	Hit	Hit	Hit	Hit	Hit	Hit	Hit	Hit	Hit

☐ Stand

▨ Hit

21

PROPOSITION BETS permit the player to increase his initial wager after he has seen his first two cards. The Proposition Bets are: (1) Double Down, (2) Split Pairs and (3) Insurance.

Rules may vary slightly in different casinos but each table has a sign that lists the Proposition Bet rules as well as wager limits. Any questions should be referred to the dealer for clarification.

Proposition bets are allowed in all casinos to permit the player to reduce his disadvantage. The player's overall disadvantage is created by those situations where both he and the dealer "break" since the player loses; it is not considered a tie. Proposition Bets may reduce this disadvantage because the player can alter his hitting strategy.

A DOUBLE DOWN BET permits the player to increase his initial wager when he wants to take only one more hit. He can add a smaller amount, but he should double his wager. The player lays his original two cards on the table as if they had been dealt face up. Then he places his Double Down wager next to his original wager (never on top of it). The dealer completes the hand by placing a single card under the wager. The typical rule allows a player to Double Down on any total but only on the original two cards dealt. Some casinos, however, may limit a Double Down to certain totals but permit it even when the player has already taken one or more "hits." A Double Down is generally allowed on totals of 11, 10 and sometimes 9.

DOUBLE DOWN

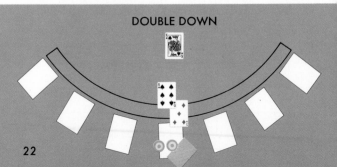

Hard Hand Strategy

PLAYER	DEALER'S CARD									
	2	3	4	5	6	7	8	9	10	A
11	■	■	■	■	■	■	■	■	■	■
10	■	■	■	■	■	■	■	■		
9	■	■	■	■	■					

■ = Double Down
□ = Do not Double Down

DOUBLING DOWN WITH HARD 11 is always recommended because the player has a chance of obtaining a "Pat" hand, 17 to 21, with no possibility of "breaking." He should Double Down with Hard 10 except when the dealer shows a 10 or Ace. The player should Double Down with Hard 10 only when the dealer's face-up card is less than the player's total of 10 because the dealer is not limited to the number of hits he may take to obtain a "Pat" hand. He should Double Down with 9 only when the dealer has a low face-up card, 2 to 6. The probability of obtaining a "Pat" hand is reduced with a Hard 9, so the player only doubles his wager when the dealer must hit.

DOUBLING DOWN WITH SOFT HANDS of 13 to 18 is recommended when the dealer has a face-up card of 4, 5 or 6 because the dealer's probability of "breaking" is at its greatest. The diagram also shows three other Soft Hand situations under which the player should Double Down.

Soft Hand Strategy

PLAYER	DEALER'S CARD									
	2	3	4	5	6	7	8	9	10	A
A-7		■	■	■	■					
A-6		■	■	■	■					
A-5			■	■	■					
A-4			■	■	■					
A-3				■	■					
A-2				■	■					

■ = Double Down
□ = Do not Double Down

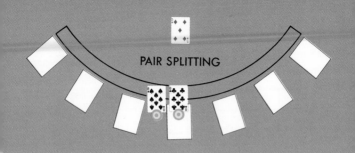

PAIR SPLITTING

PAIR SPLITTING is allowed when a player is dealt two cards of equal value. Most casinos permit the pair to be split into two independent hands. The player turns his pair face up and separates the two cards. He tucks one under his original wager and lays the other card next to it. Then he must place an equal wager on the second card. The player plays out both hands, beginning with the card to the right. The right hand must be completed first, because the player cannot return to it after he draws to the left card. The player indicates his choices with the hand signals that are used for face-up cards.

IN COMPLETING A SPLIT PAIR, the player has several options available. Once he has drawn to a card from the original pair to produce a new hand of two cards:

a) The player may hit or stand.

b) In addition, some casinos permit a Double Down according to the established rules.

c) If the first card drawn to either hand produces another pair, many casinos permit it to be split.

d) Casinos usually allow a maximum of four hands to be created from the original pair. (There are 12 face cards in a single deck and at least 16 of every value card in a four deck shoe.)

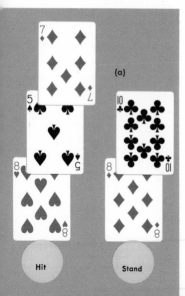

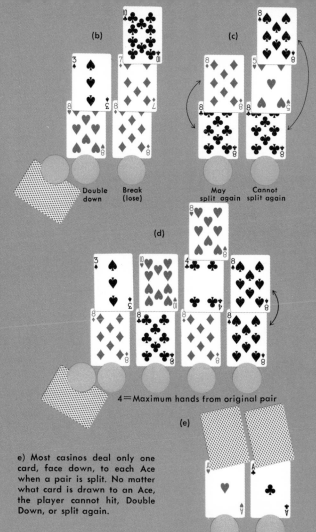

(b)

Double down

Break (lose)

(c)

May split again

Cannot split again

(d)

4 = Maximum hands from original pair

(e)

e) Most casinos deal only one card, face down, to each Ace when a pair is split. No matter what card is drawn to an Ace, the player cannot hit, Double Down, or split again.

Only one hit to split aces

P L A Y E R	DEALER'S CARD									
	2	3	4	5	6	7	8	9	10	A
A-A	■	■	■	■	■	■	■	■	■	■
10-10										
9-9	■	■	■	■	■		■	■		
8-8	■	■	■	■	■	■	■	■	■	■
7-7	■	■	■	■	■	■				
6-6	■	■	■	■	■					
5-5										
4-4				■	■					
3-3	■	■	■	■	■	■				
2-2	■	■	■	■	■	■				

■ Split pair   ☐ Do not split pair

PAIR SPLITTING STRATEGY is not complicated. Aces should always be split even though casinos usually permit only one card to each Ace. After a split, an Ace and a 10 value card equal 21, but they are not treated as Blackjack. Such a hand wins and pays 1 to 1 except when the dealer also obtains 21 to tie. A pair of eights should also be split. Hitting to two hands of 8 is not especially good but it is always better than one wager on 16. A pair of 10's is never split because it is better to stand on a total of 20. A pair of 5's is never split because it is better to hit or Double Down on 10. It is better to hit one hand of 8 than to split 4's, except when the dealer's hand shows a 5. The rest of the pairs, 2, 3, 6, 7 and 9 are split only when the dealer has a low face-up card.

INSURANCE is a bet offered by most casinos when the dealer's face-up card is an Ace. After the initial two cards are dealt to each player, and before any cards are drawn, the dealer interrupts the game and asks, "Insurance?" The players are given time to look at their cards and make the wager. The Insurance wager, which can be a maximum of one-half of the amount of the original wager, is placed directly in front of the player in the Insurance bet area. Then the dealer looks at his Hole card, and if he does not have Blackjack, the Insurance bet is lost and play continues. However, when the dealer has a 10 value card in the Hole to produce Blackjack, the Insurance bet wins and pays the player 2 to 1, the amount of his original wager.

THE DECISION to take Insurance, contrary to popular belief, is made completely independent of the two-card total in the player's hand. The only relevant factor is the probability of the dealer having a 10 in the Hole. The player should never take Insurance, no matter what his first two cards are, unless he is keeping track of the discards and he knows at least one-third of the cards remaining in the deck are 10's.

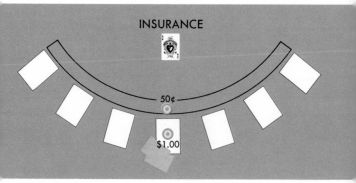

INSURANCE

50¢

$1.00

SURRENDERING THE HAND before taking a "hit" is sometimes allowed. Some casinos permit the player to cancel his hand before he draws any cards by surrendering one-half of his wager. However, it is an extremely rare hand in which the player does not have at least one-quarter chance of winning, but in that rare case it is better to give the casino one-half of the wager than to risk losing all of it.

TWO OR MORE HANDS can be wagered on in each deal but casinos usually require more than the minimum wager for each hand. The player cannot touch the cards in a hand until he has completed the hand to the right of it except when the dealer has an Ace face up. Then the player may look at each hand to decide if he wants to take Insurance. The beginner should not complicate the situation by playing more than one hand.

It should be emphasized that the opportunity of winning is the same at every betting location. There is a popular belief among players that Third Base, the position to the far left of the table, influences what cards the dealer will draw; however, the third baseman's strategy decisions do not have any overall effects on the dealer's hand.

CARD COUNTING is the most effective strategy for playing Twenty-One. When the dealer begins a new hand without shuffling after the completion of the previous hand, the composition of the deck is different from the standard 52-card deck he began with. This changes the probabilities of the hand totals which are possible on the next deal. By counting the discards after each hand, the player can exploit those situations in which he has a greater opportunity of winning by increasing the amount of his wager. He can also improve his playing strategy according to the remaining cards.

Card counting is an effective playing strategy. It can reduce the casino advantage to a minimum.

Many casino executives and players are convinced that counting gives the player an advantage over the casino, but this has not been proven. There is still no agreement on how much advantage a casino has when a player uses basic strategy, and this percent would be easier to calculate than the casino advantage when the player uses a counting strategy.

EFFECTIVE COUNTING requires the player to keep track of all cards, alter his wager according to the probability of each situation, and adjust his playing strategy to the changing situation; a great deal of concentration is required to insure accuracy.

WHEN HIGH CARDS have been discarded from the deck, an excess of low cards remain. Having a greater number of low cards increases the probability that the dealer will win, because low cards increase the chance of the dealer obtaining a "Pat" hand, 17 to 21, when he must hit a Stiff, 12 to 16. In such case, low cards work to the dealer's advantage. An abundance of low cards works against the player, since his best strategy is to draw according to the dealer's fixed hitting rules and attempt to obtain a "Pat" hand of his own. Unfortunately, this strategy increases the possibility that the player will "break", so the casino advantage becomes even greater. In addition, extra low cards restrict the opportunity to Double Down, since the player is less likely to draw a high card.

WHEN LOW CARDS have been discarded from the deck, leaving an excess of high cards, it increases the probability that the player will win. High cards increase the likelihood of achieving Blackjack and improve the player's chance of obtaining a high card on a Double Down. Both dealer and player will be dealt the same proportion of hand totals in the long run, but in those partially used decks that contain an excess of high cards, the player can obtain the advantage by using the proper hitting strategy. The player should stop hitting Stiffs, 12 to 16, because the probability is too high that he will draw a high card and "break." Thus, when both the player and dealer have a Stiff, the player stands and lets the dealer hit. When many high cards remain in the deck, the dealer will often draw one and "break."

COUNTING STRATEGIES are beyond the scope of this book, except to explain the principle on which each is based.

ACE-COUNT is the most obvious strategy because Aces are essential to achieve Blackjack and they make the most favorable pair to split; it is not the best strategy. As the relative number of Aces remaining in the deck increases, the player can only alter the size of his wager, but not his playing strategy.

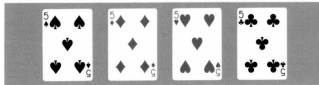

A 5-COUNT is more effective than Ace count, because the player can alter not only the size of his wager but his playing strategy, as 5's are dealt from the deck. Anytime the dealer must hit a Stiff, 12 to 16 a 5 gives him a "Pat" hand, 17 to 21. When the 5's have been discarded from the deck, there is a greater probability the dealer will "break."

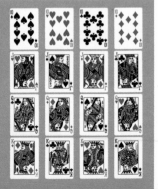

A 10-COUNT is even more effective because there are four times as many 10 value cards. Even though the removal of each individual 10 from the deck does not influence the advantage as much as each 5 or Ace, 10's are more important as a group. The 10-count is more accurate than the previous counts because it is more sensitive to the changes in probabilities as each card is dealt. The 10-count helps the player to make more subtle variations in both his playing strategy and the size of his wagers. He can take Insurance when it is to his advantage because this counting strategy indicates when there are more than one-third 10's remaining in the deck.

NUMBER COUNT is the most effective strategy of all because it considers the influence of every card remaining in the deck. Each card value is given a number which equals its relative importance to the casino advantage. For example, the 2's through 7's might be each given a value of $+1$ and the 9's, 10's and Aces a value of -1. As each card is played from the deck, the number, which represents the card, is either added or subtracted from the running total depending on whether it is to the player's or the dealer's advantage to have it removed from the deck. In this example, each time a low card is dealt, the player would add 1 and each time a high card is dealt, subtract 1.

In using a number count, the player must either count the number of cards remaining in the deck, or estimate them, because the amount of the running total reflects a different casino advantage depending on the number of cards in the deck. Third Base is the best seat for a sophisticated counter because he can adjust his hitting strategy according to the cards dealt to other customers.

A SIMPLE NUMBER COUNT, as in the example above, has only one positive number for each low card removed from the deck and the same but negative number for each high card removed from the deck. The High-Low Number Count usually makes 8 or else 7, 8 and 9 neutral. They have a minor effect and have the value of 0.

A COMPLEX NUMBER COUNT assigns a number to every card value which is added and subtracted in the same manner. The player must remember different numbers for each card value. This is the most comprehensive and effective method of analyzing the entire deck to determine the proper size of the wager and the best playing strategy.

CRAPS

Craps provides faster and more exciting action than any of the other casino games. There are few players who are familiar with all the rules and practices of the game, and even fewer who know the correct odds on each betting option. There is no way to win in the long run, but one can learn more about the game and reduce his rate of loss.

A Crap layout usually has three sections. The two outside sections are identical so it does not matter which end of the table a person plays. All players at the table may wager on the Proposition Bets in the center of the layout. A Crap table usually operates with four employees: the Boxman, two dealers, and the Stickman.

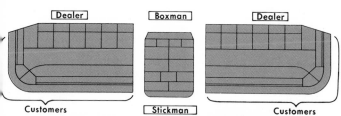

THE BOXMAN sits at the center of the layout and drops all currency into the money box. He directs the game and watches the dice, money, chips, dealers, players, and all transactions.

THE STICKMAN stands in the center of the player's side of the table. The Stickman is responsible for the handling of the dice and the Proposition Bets, located in the center of the layout.

TWO DEALERS stand, one on each side of the Boxman. They collect the losing wagers and each pays off the winning wagers on his side of the table. Dealers also make change for the players.

NOTE: In this section on Craps, the numbers which represent dice totals are always printed in red to distinguish them from numbers for other quantities which appear in black.

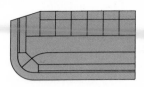

CHANGE CAN BE OBTAINED by a player if he places his currency in front of the dealer and calls out, "change". The dealer will usually repeat, "change," particularly if the dealer must handle wagers first. The dealer hands the money to the Boxman, who counts it and tells the dealer the amount. Then the dealer places an equivalent amount in chips on the layout directly in front of the player. Chips should never be left on the table unless they are wagered in the betting areas because they get in the way of the dice. These chips may also be mistaken as a wager. The player should place all other chips in the grooves provided at the top of the table railing directly in front of him.

When the player quits with a lot of chips, he can have them exchanged for larger value chips so that he will have fewer to carry. When he hands his chips in, he requests a "color change" because each chip value is a different color.

It is well to remember that dealers are required to pay off all winning wagers from the previous roll of the dice before they can make change. Dealers also usually set up wagers for players who have chips before they make change.

PASS LINE BET

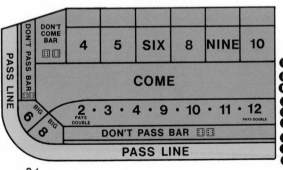

34

THE PASS LINE BET is the most popular bet in Craps, even though the Don't Pass bet, to be explained later, offers the player a lower casino advantage.

THE FIRST ROLL of the dice for the Pass Line is called the Come-out roll. On the Come-out, the player wins if a Natural 7 or 11 appears and loses if a crap 2, 3 or 12 appears. If one of the remaining six totals—4, 5, 6, 8, 9 or 10 appears, it becomes the Pass Line Point. When a Point is rolled on the Come-out, both dealers place a round Point marker directly in front of them in the Point box that has that number printed on it.

ON THE POINT ROLL, new rules determine whether the Pass Line wins or loses. The bet wins only if that Point (indicated by Point marker) appears again and loses only if 7 appears. No matter how many rolls it takes, no other number affects the wager, which must remain on the bet until either the Point or 7 appears. A Pass Line win pays 1 to 1. The dealer places an equal amount in chips next to the player's wager.

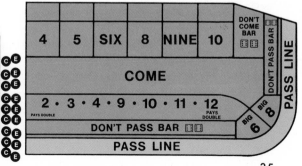

COME-OUT ROLL VS. POINT ROLL

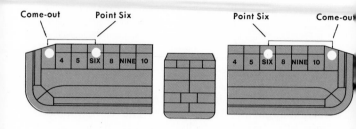

THE COME-OUT ROLL is the first roll of the dice by the first player to bet at an empty table. The Come-out roll rules are also applied to every roll which follows a winning or losing decision on the Pass Line. For example, when a Come-out roll wins (Natural 7 or 11) or loses (Crap 2, 3 or 12), the next roll is another Come-out. Similarly, when a Point roll wins (Point appears) or loses (7 appears), the next roll is a Come-out.

At a table that has been empty or after a decision on the Pass Line, the dealers set the Point marker on each side of the layout aside. The dealers generally place the Point marker in the Don't Come Bet box, but they always completely remove it from the location of the six Point boxes. A dealer does not place his marker in a Point box until one of the six Point numbers, for example 6, appears on a Come-out roll to become the Point. The dealer does not move the marker back to the Come-out location until the Point appears, in this example 6, and the player wins or until 7 appears and the player loses. A new Come-out roll is then in order.

THE PLAYER'S ADVANTAGE on the Come-out roll is greater than the casino's because there will be an average of 8 Naturals to every 4 Craps. There will be an average of 12 decisions (wins and loses) out of every 36 Come-out rolls. The other 24 rolls will be Points. However, the casino more than compensates for the player's initial advantage once a Point is established because the casino wins on 7 which appears more often than any of the other dice totals. Once a Point is established, the player cannot remove his Pass Line wager unless it wins. If the player were allowed to remove his wager, he would be able to retain his initial advantage over the casino and wager only on the Come-out rolls.

All bets except the Pass Line and Come, can be removed by the player at any time. The player has the right to wager on the Pass Line on any roll, but he should never make or increase a Pass Line wager on a Point roll because the casino advantage is very high after a Point has been established because 7 is so likely to appear. The player should only make a Pass Line wager on a Come-out roll.

COME BET

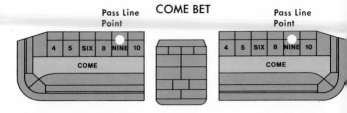

Pass Line Point   Pass Line Point

THE COME BET wins and loses according to the rules for the Pass Line bet on page 35. The Pass Line bet should be made only on Come-out rolls and the Come Bet only when a Point has been established on the Pass Line (when the Point marker is in one of the Point boxes). The player may make a Come wager on each and every Point roll. A Come wager wins on the next roll if a Natural 7 or 11 appears and loses if a Craps 2, 3 or 12 appears.

WHEN A COME POINT, 4, 5, 6, 8, 9 or 10 appears, the dealer moves the player's wager to that Point box, for example 4. A Come wager in a Point box wins if that Point number appears, in this example 4, and loses if 7 appears. A Come wager cannot be removed from a Point box until it either wins or loses. All wagers at the Craps table, except the Pass Line and Come, can be removed by the player at any

COME POINT

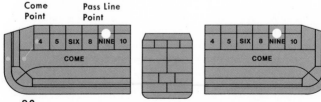

Come Point   Pass Line Point

COME PAYOFF

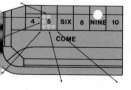 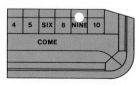

time. When a Point has been established and a 7 appears, the Pass Line bet and all Come wagers in Point boxes lose, but a wager in the Come Bet wins because it is its first roll on the table.

PAYOFFS FOR COME BETS are placed next to the player's wager by the dealer when a Come Bet wins on the first roll. When a Come Bet is in a Point box and it wins because that Point total appears, the dealer moves the player's wager back to the Come Bet and places the payoff chips next to it. The Come Bet always pays 1 to 1. The player's wager and the payoff become the wager on the next roll unless the player alters the amount.

THE PLAYER'S LOCATION around the table indicates where his wager will be placed in the Point box so that there is no question about ownership.

CUSTOMER POINT BOX LOCATION

 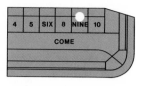

DON'T PASS BET

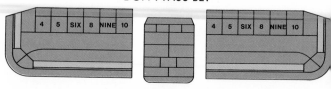

THE DON'T PASS AND DON'T COME BETS have the lowest casino advantage of all crap bets. However, the Pass Line and Come are much more popular bets because of tradition and lack of knowledge. They lose at an average rate of 12¢ more, for each $1,000 wagered, than the Don't Pass and Don't Come Bets. The Don't Pass Bet is basically the opposite of the Pass Line Bet. With one exception, when one wins, the other loses.

ON THE COME-OUT ROLL the player loses on Natural 7 or 11 and wins on Craps 2 or 3, but not on Crap 12. In the Don't Pass and Don't Come betting boxes the picture of the dice shows Barred 12. This means that Crap 12 is a tie (neither wins or loses) and no money changes hands. After a Barred total appears the player may change the amount of his bet or remove it completely.

THE DON'T PASS BET cannot be the exact opposite of the Pass Line Bet because the player would have the advantage. When Crap 12, which appears on an average of once in every 36 rolls, is Barred, it changes a Pass Line win into a tie. This single difference is enough to give the casino almost the same advantage on both the Pass Line and the Don't Pass Bets.

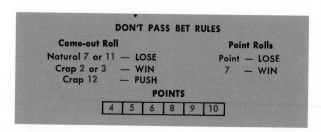

DON'T PASS BET RULES

Come-out Roll		Point Rolls	
Natural 7 or 11	— LOSE	Point	— LOSE
Crap 2 or 3	— WIN	7	— WIN
Crap 12	— PUSH		

POINTS

4	5	6	8	9	10

DON'T PASS BET CASINO ADVANTAGE

COME-OUT ROLL

Naturals			Craps		
Dice Total	Number of Rolls		Dice Total	Number of Rolls	
7	=	6	2	=	1
11	=	2	3	=	2
	LOSE 8	— Customer —		WIN 3	

POINT ROLLS

	WIN	LOSE	
Dice Total	Number of Rolls	Dice Total	Customer Advantage
	⎧ 6 to 3 = 4 or 10		33.3%
7	= ⎨ 6 to 4 = 5 or 9		20.0%
	⎩ 6 to 5 = 6 or 8		9.1%

A DON'T PASS WAGER on the Come-out roll results in a large casino advantage over the player. In every 36 Come-outs, he will win an average of only 3 wagers while losing 8. However, the casino advantage is reduced once a point is established because the player wins on 7 which appears more often than the other numbers. When a player has a point on the Don't Pass, he has a large advantage over the casino. The Don't Pass and Don't Come are the only bets which the player cannot make or add to once a point has been established because he has the advantage. However, the casino will permit the player to remove his Don't wagers at any time because the player gives up this strong advantage. Obviously, this should never be done. This rule is the opposite of the Pass Line and Come Bet rules which permit the player to make a wager at any time but prohibit him from removing it once a Point has been established. These are the only restrictions on adding and removing wagers. Every other bet allows the player the option of adding to his wager or removing it on every roll of the dice.

41

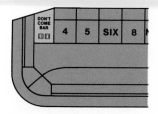 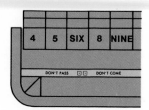

IN LAS VEGAS, the Don't Come Bet is located at the back corners of the layout. The player should stand near this location when he makes Don't Come wagers so he does not have to reach a long distance to place his wagers and retrieve his winnings.

CRAP 12 IS BARRED on the Don't Bets in Las Vegas, but in Reno-Tahoe, Crap 2 is usually Barred. Since Craps 2 and 12 have the same probability of occurrence—1 in every 36 rolls—this change does not affect the casino advantage. However, it does affect

IN RENO-TAHOE the Don't Come parallels the Pass Line around the entire layout. These layouts do not have a Don't Pass Bet, so a player who wants to wager on either the Don't Pass or Don't Come, always wagers on the Don't Come Bet.

the specific numbers on which the player wins and Pushes. In some areas Crap 3 is Barred. This increases the casino advantage because Crap 3 appears twice as often as either Craps 2 or 12. Any Don't Bet is relatively bad with a Barred Crap 3.

THE DON'T COME BET has the same win, lose and Barred rules as the Don't Pass, and except for the Barred number, it has the opposite rules of the Come Bet. The player may make a Don't Come wager on each and every Point Roll.

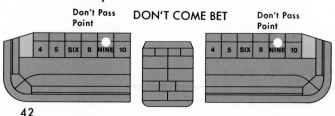

DON'T COME BET

Don't Pass Point

Don't Pass Point

DON'T COME POINT BET

Don't Come Point   Don't Pass Point

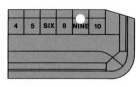

WHEN A POINT—4, 5, 6, 8, 9 or 10 appears, the dealer moves the wager to the box above that Point number. A Don't Come wager wins if Craps 2 or 3 appears, loses if Natural 7 or 11 appears, and Ties if Barred 12 appears. The Don't Come Point boxes do not have any printing in them, but the player should imagine 7 in each one because the player wins when 7 appears and loses if the Point number appears.

contained in the box below it appears, in this example 4. When a player has several Don't Come wagers in the Don't Come Point boxes, he loses only one at a time as the respective Points appear, but he wins them all at once when 7 appears. However, when 7 does appear the player loses the wager in the Don't Come Bet because it is treated according to the Come-out roll rules.

PAYOFFS FOR DON'T COME BETS are placed next to the player's wager when a Don't Come Bet wins on the first roll. When a Don't Come wager is in a Don't Come Point box, it wins when 7 appears. The dealer moves the player's wager back to the Don't Come Bet and places the payoff chips next to

it. When the player has wagers in more than one Don't Come Point box, the dealer pays them off in the boxes and piles the entire amount in the Don't Come Bet. The Don't Come Bet always pays 1 to 1. All chips remain in the Don't Come box as the wager for the next roll unless the player changes the amount.

Payoff

DON'T COME PAYOFF

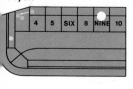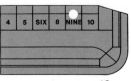

THE STICKMAN controls the dice, which he keeps in a bowl in front of him. He usually has 5 to 8 dice which he offers to a player. The player selects any 2 dice he desires and immediately picks them up and throws them past the Stickman to the other end of the table. They should be thrown aggressively because they must bounce against the other end of the table. After each roll, the Stickman announces the total and then pulls the dice with a long stick to the center of the table in front of the Boxman. When the dealers have collected and paid all wagers, the Stickman shoves the pair of dice to the player, who immediately picks them up and shoots them again.

A player must wager on either the Pass Line or the Don't Pass when he shoots the dice. In addition, he may make any other wagers he desires. All other players can also wager on any bet or combination of bets they want. The shooter only loses the dice when he throws 7 on a Point roll. The shooter cannot lose them on a Come-out roll, and he does not lose them on a Point roll unless 7 appears. When a player's turn shooting is complete, the Stickman offers all of the dice in the bowl to the next player in a clockwise direction.

When a player has the dice, he should always keep them in view of the Stickman. If the dice are concealed from view, the Stickman must call them in to be examined by the Boxman. The player is then offered another pair of dice from the bowl. If the player continues to remove the dice from view, he is prohibited from shooting them. If the player does not want to shoot the dice, he waves his hand toward the left, and the Stickman then offers them to the next player.

The author shooting dice at Las Vegas Hilton

THE DICE are out of play and the roll is nullified if
one or both of the dice bounce off the table. The
Stickman announces, "No roll!" and offers the remaining dice to the player to select another pair.
No money is collected or paid out, and the players
may change their wagers. When both dice land on
the table the roll always counts unless a die lands
in the dice bowl or lands on the stacks of chips which
are stored in front of the Boxman or in the metal
racks that some casinos place in front of the dealers.

THE ODDS BET is the only bet which does not give the casino an advantage. In the long run, the casino will not come out ahead of the players. Odds is offered by the casino as a courtesy bet to stimulate wagering on the Pass Line, Come, Don't Pass and Don't Come Bets. These four bets have a low casino advantage, and the addition of Odds makes them even more attractive. Wagering the Odds Bets should be the principal objective of the Crap player because the casino does not expect to profit. Odds can be wagered only on the Point rolls of these four bets.

AN ODDS WAGER may be put behind the player's Pass Line wager when a Point, for example 5, is established. Both wagers win when the Point appears, in this example 5, and both wagers lose when 7 appears. When the wagers win, the Pass Line wager is paid off 1 to 1, but the Odds wager is paid off by the ratio of the probability of 7 to the probability of the Point. In this example, 5 is paid off 3 to 2. After the wagers win, the Odds wager must be removed because Odds can only be taken on Point rolls, and the next roll is a Come-out. A wager on the Pass Line, Come, Don't Pass or Don't Come is called a "Flat" wager because the payoff is 1 to 1. The stack of chips for the payoff is the same height as the wager; the wager is paid off "Flat." This terminology distinguishes a Flat wager and an Odds wager on the same bet because Odds wagers are always paid off at a ratio of more than 1 to 1.

ODDS BET ON PASS LINE

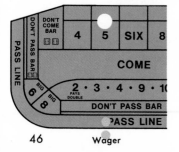

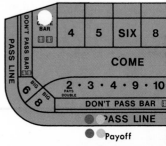

46   Wager   Payoff

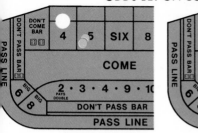 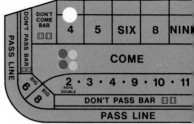

Wager   Payoff

ODDS ON A COME WAGER may be made when the
Come wager has been moved to a Point box. The
player puts his Odds wager on the Come and identifies the Point to the dealer, for example "Odds on
5." The dealer then sets the Odds wager on top of
the player's Come wager. The Odds wager is set
slightly forward on the Come wager because the
two wagers receive different payoffs. If 7 appears
both wagers lose. If the Point appears, in this
example 5, both wagers win. The dealer moves both
wagers back to the Come Bet and pays them off.
The Come wager is paid 1 to 1, and the Odds wager
is paid off by the ratio of the probability of 7 to
the probability of the Point. In this example, the
Point 5 pays 3 to 2. All of the chips (the two wagers
and the two payoffs) remain on the Come for the
next roll unless the player removes all or part of
them. The player should watch his Odds wagers
closely and make sure the dealer places them
properly on the Come wagers. If the player always
wagers the correct amount of Odds after each point
is rolled, the dealer will expect the wager and no
further conversation between the two is necessary.

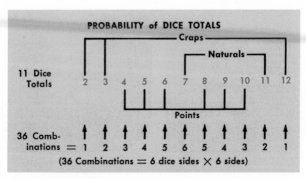

PROBABILITY of DICE TOTALS

Craps

Naturals

11 Dice Totals: 2 3 4 5 6 7 8 9 10 11 12

Points

36 Combinations = 1 2 3 4 5 6 5 4 3 2 1

(36 Combinations = 6 dice sides × 6 sides)

THE PROBABILITY RATIO of the appearance of 7 to that of the appearance of each of the 6 Points—4, 5, 6, 8, 9 or 10, is the best basis for Odds Bets. A pair of dice produces 36 different combinations (6 sides × 6 sides = 36 combinations), but only 11 dice totals, 2 through 12. In each series of 36 roles these 11 totals do not have the same probability of appearing. For example, 7 appears 6 times while 2 and 12 each only appear once. Odds Bets are created when 2 of these probabilities are combined into a ratio. A 7 is produced by 6 combinations of the dice, but the Points are produced by only 3, 4 or 5 combinations.

ODDS RATIOS		
Total	Payoff	Totals
7 =	6 to 3	= 4 or 10
7 =	6 to 4	= 5 or 9
7 =	6 to 5	= 6 or 8

Therefore, when a player has a Pass Line or a Come wager and a Point is established, he loses more often than he wins because 7 appears more often than each of the Points.

When the Point does appear, the Flat wager is paid 1 to 1, but the Odds wager is paid 6 to 3 for Points 4 and 10, 6 to 4 for Points 5 and 9, and 6 to 5 for Points 6 and 8.

THE ODDS PAYOFFS equal the probability of the Point losing to a 7. For example, 7 is produced by 6 combinations, but Point 4 is produced by only 3 combinations in each series of 36 rolls. With Point 4, the Odds Bet will lose an average of 6 times for every 3 times it wins. But, when 4 appears, the Odds Bet is paid off 6 to 3. This payoff compensates the player for the greater number of losses with Point 4. The casino and players break even in the long run; there is no casino advantage.

SINGLE ODDS means that the player cannot wager more on Odds than the amount of his Flat wager. Odds Bets, which have no casino advantage, are offered to stimulate wagering on the Pass Line, Come, Don't Pass and Don't Come. Casinos do not make any profit on Odds Bets so they restrict the size of Odds wagers to a proportion of the amount of the Flat wager.

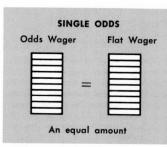

SINGLE ODDS

Odds Wager   Flat Wager

An equal amount

SOME CASINOS permit wagers which are larger than Single Odds. The player should always inquire what the ratio of the Odds wager to the Flat wager is, so that he can take the maximum amount of Odds that are permitted.

FULL ODDS offered by most casinos let the player wager a greater amount than Single Odds on Points 5, 6, 8 and 9 in those situations when the correct payoff cannot be calculated for Single Odds. The Points 4 and 10 each pay 2 to 1. Any wager made in multiples of the table minimum may be correctly paid off so Single Odds remains in effect. The Points 5 and 9 each pay 3 to 2. Wagers made with an even amount of chips can be correctly paid off, 3 chips for every 2 chips. However, when an odd amount of chips is wagered, the correct payoff of 3 to 2 includes one-half of the table minimum. For example, for a $1.00 wager a 3 to 2 payoff is $1.50, and for a $3.00 wager a 3 to 2 payoff is $4.50, etc. Casinos usually do not make payoffs which are not in multiples of the table minimum. In this example, at a $1.00 minimum table, the extra $.50 in each 3 to 2 payoff would have to be canceled.

FULL ODDS		
Totals	Payoffs	Amount of Odds Wager
4 or 10	2 to 1	Equals amount of Flat wager
5 or 9	3 to 2	Next even amount of chips
6 or 8	6 to 5	Nearest multiple of 5 chips

A FLAT WAGER that is an odd amount of chips on a Point of 5 or 9, may be remedied by adding one chip to the Odds wager to make it an even amount of chips. If the player has a Flat wager of 3 $5.00 chips, for a total of $15.00, he can add the table minimum, a $1.00 chip, to create an even wager of $16.00, or he can add another chip of the denomination he is wagering, $5.00 for a total of $20.00. A chip of the denomination he is wagering will add more money to the layout with no casino advantage.

The Points 6 and 8 pay 6 to 5. The correct Odds payoff can be made only if the player wagers multiples of 5 chips, i.e., 5, 10, 15, etc. When the player has a Flat wager of 1 or 2 chips over a multiple of 5, he wagers the previous multiple of 5. For example, if he has a Flat wager of 2 chips, he may not make an Odds wager. If he has a Flat wager of 7 chips (5 + 2) he is 2 chips over the previous multiple of 5 chips, which is all he can wager on the Odds Bet that will be paid 6 to 5.

When the player has a Flat wager of 3 or 4 chips over a multiple of 5, he can wager the next multiple of 5. For example, if he has a Flat wager of 3 chips, he may make an Odds wager of 5 chips. If he has a Flat wager of 8 chips (5 + 3) he is 3 chips over the previous multiple of 5 chips, so he may wager the next multiple of 5, with 10 chips on the Odds Bet.

Some casinos may offer a few more variations on Single Odds. The player will have to inquire at each casino about these opportunities to obtain Odds Bets which are even larger in comparison to the Flat Bets.

The Odds wagers should always be made in multiples for correct payoffs or the casino will pay 1 to 1 on the short multiples. The 3 to 2 payoff becomes only 2 to 2 and the 6 to 5 payoff becomes only 5 to 5 for partial multiples. When the player has a short multiple, he may be tempted to add chips to his Flat wager so he can increase his Odds wager to the next payoff multiple. This should never be done, as a Flat wager has a large disadvantage once a Point has been established; the increased Odds wager, which has no advantage, cannot compensate for this greater disadvantage.

THE MAXIMUM PROPORTION of odds is obtained when the player makes a Flat wager of 3 chips. The amount of the Odds wager is determined by the amount of the Flat wager. Therefore, the player should only make his Flat wagers in amounts which permit him to maximize the amount he wagers on his Odds Bets.

When the player makes a Flat wager of 3 chips, the Odds wager should also be 3 chips for Points 4 and 10, 4 chips for Points 5 and 9, and 5 chips for Points 6 and 8. The payoff is always 6 chips for the Odds wager and 3 chips for the Flat wager. If the player wagers the table minimum, 1 chip, he should take Odds of 1 chip on the Points 4 and 10, and Odds of 2 chips on 5 and 9. He cannot take Odds on 6 and 8 because Odds requires a Flat wager of at least 3 chips.

MAXIMIZING FULL ODDS

Flat Wager = 1 Chip			Flat Wager = 3 Chips		
Odds Wager	Totals	Payoff	Odds Wager	Totals	Payoff
1 Chip	4 or 10	2 to 1	3 Chips	4 or 10	6 to 3
2 Chips	5 or 9	3 to 2	4 Chips	5 or 9	6 to 4
0 Chips	6 or 8	0	5 Chips	6 or 8	6 to 5

DOUBLE ODDS means that the player can wager twice as much on Odds as he wagers Flat. Unfortunately, Double Odds is rarely offered by casinos. The player obtains the maximum proportion of Odds, under this rule, when he makes a Flat wager of 5 chips and makes an Odds wager of 10 chips on each Point. Some casinos that offer Double Odds will pay 5 to 2 on the Points 6 and 8. In these casinos the player should make Flat wagers in amounts of 2 or 4 chips and make Odds wagers of 5 or 10 chips respectively on the Points of 6 and 8.

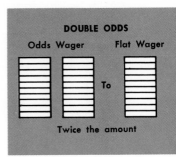

DOUBLE ODDS

Odds Wager   Flat Wager

To

Twice the amount

THE ODDS, PLACE, AND BUY WAGERS all lose when 7 appears, but, on Come-out rolls, the Pass Line wins when 7 appears. Most players are oriented to the Pass Line so they remove their Odds, Place and Buy wagers on Come-outs.

The removal of wagers (Odds, Place and Buy) does not influence the player's expectations because the likelihood of 7 remains constant on every roll. It would waste time to remove all of these wagers on Come-out rolls and replace them again on Point rolls. The Odds, Place and Buy wagers are left on the layout on Come-out rolls, but they are "off" which means that they do not win and do not lose. If a Point appears, a Come wager wins and is paid off, but the Odds wager on top of it is returned to the player with no payoff. If 7 appears, the Come wager loses and is collected, but the Odds wager is still returned to the player.

If the player wants these wagers to win and lose on every roll of the dice, he tells the dealer that his wagers "work" on Come-out rolls. The dealer will either place the Point marker or a small "On" button on the player's wager.

BETS "ON" ON COME-OUT ROLL

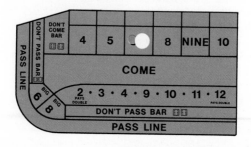

ODDS BET ON DON'T PASS

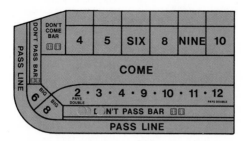

ODDS ON THE DON'T PASS may be laid on Point rolls. The principle of Odds is the same as for the Pass Line but the terminology is different. On the Pass Line and Come, the player may "take" Odds, and on the Don't Pass and Don't Come, the player may "lay" Odds. The player lays his Odds wager next to his Flat wager by tilting all of the chips off the edge of the bottom chip.

ODDS ON A DON'T COME wager can be laid after it has been moved to a Don't Come Point box. The player puts his Odds wager on the Don't Come Bet and identifies the Point, for example, "Lay the 5." The dealer lays the Odds next to the Flat wager. If the Point appears, both wagers lose. If 7 appears, both wagers win. The dealer moves both wagers, along with the payoffs, to the Don't Come Bet. Unlike Odds wagers in Come Point boxes, Odds wagers in Don't Come Point boxes always work even on Come-out rolls.

ODDS BET ON DON'T COME

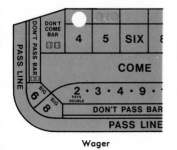

Wager   Payoff   53

FULL ODDS for DON'T BETS	
Totals	Payoff
4 or 10	1 to 2
5 or 9	2 to 3
6 or 8	5 to 6

FULL ODDS FOR DON'T PASS BETS

FULL ODDS FOR DON'T PASS BETS have the same, but reversed, payoff ratios of the Odds Bets on the Do Pass Line. For example, a Pass Line Odds wager on Point 4 is paid off 2 to 1, while a Don't Pass Odds wager on Point 4 is paid off 1 to 2. When one wins, the other loses.

When the player lays the Odds on the Don't Pass, the Odds payoff is always less than the amount of his Odds wager because he wins more often than he loses, 7 appears more often than any Point. The player has a greater probability of winning so he is paid proportionately less. The casino and players break even in the long run; there is no casino advantage.

MAXIMIZING FULL ODDS for Don't bets is always desirable. When the Don't Pass and the Pass Line have the same size Flat wager, the amount of the Don't Pass Full Odds wager is the payoff for a Pass Line Full Odds wager. The Don't Pass Full Odds payoff ratios are the reverse of the Do Full Odds payoff ratios on Page 51. The player calculates the amount of the Full Odds wager and its payoff for a Pass Line wager of the same size and then he wagers that payoff on Don't Pass Odds. If the player wagers the table minimum, 1 chip, he should lay Odds of 2 chips on Points 4 and 10 and lay Odds of 3 chips on 5 and 9. The player cannot lay Odds on 6 and 8 because a Flat wager of at least 3 units is required. The player obtains the maximum proportions of Odds when he makes a Flat Wager of 3 chips. The player lays Odds of 6 chips on all Points, and he wins 3 chips for Points 4 and 10, wins 4 chips for 5 and 9, and wins 5 chips for 6 and 8.

MAXIMIZING FULL ODDS for DON'T BETS

Flat Wager = 1 Chip			Flat Wager = 3 Chips		
Odds Wager	Totals	Payoff	Odds Wager	Totals	Payoff
2 Chips	4 or 10	1 to 2	6 Chips	4 or 10	3 to 6
3 Chips	5 or 9	2 to 3	6 Chips	5 or 9	4 to 6
0 Chips	6 or 8	0	6 Chips	6 or 8	5 to 6

(1) A beginner should make only one bet at a time so he will not be confused by the speed of the game. He should start by making a Pass Line wager; and once he is comfortable with it, he should add Odds on the Point rolls.

(2) Next, he makes wagers on the Come Bet and learns to take Odds on it. Finally, the customer, who wants to get the most action, will make wagers on the Pass Line or Come Bet on every roll with Full Odds.

(3) The Don't Bets are also learned systematically. The beginner should make only a Don't Pass wager and then lay the Odds. Next, he would make a Don't Come wager and lay the Odds. Practice will develop his ability to wager on every roll of his choice.

(4) The customer should make only those Craps Bets which have already been discussed—the DO Bets (Pass Line and Come), which are the most popular on the layout, or the DON'T Bets (Don't Pass and Don't Come), which have the lowest casino advantage. In addition, the customer should always take or lay Full Odds on Point rolls.

(5) The customer should have a thorough understanding of what he is doing before he wagers. He should know the amount and location of each of his wagers. He should also know where the dealer will move them on the layout, as well as the amount and location of the payoff.

(6) The customer is responsible for his own money. If he has more wagers on the table than he can follow, he may not notice a mistake made by the dealer, or by another customer who mistakenly picks up his wager.

(7) The customer should make himself clearly understood, and should ask questions about anything he does not understand. The dealer will quickly learn the customer's pattern and expect his next wager, so the customer should make his intentions known when he alters his normal pattern of play.

(8) The customer must complain immediately if he is unhappy about any situation because the next roll of the dice will eliminate the grounds of the claim. Legitimate claims are almost always settled to the satisfaction of the customer.

NOTE: The Following pages (56-77) come under the heading, **CRAPS IN OPERATION** and illustrate the game as it is actually played in a series of throws of the dice.

Craps in operation is illustrated in detail with a succession of table layouts found on pages 58 through 77. The left section of each layout contains "DO" wagers with "FULL ODDS," and the right section contains "DON'T" wagers with "FULL ODDS." The similarities and differences of the DO and DON'T wagers can be observed and studied in detail by comparing both sections.

The two center wagers have three chips each, and both side wagers have only one chip each. By following one of these wagers through the series of layouts, the proper ratio for FULL ODDS can be learned very quickly.

A color and graphic representation have been used to identify and to differentiate the wagers from the payoffs:

▶ Yellow chips represent new customer wagers made for the current roll of the dice, while orange chips represent existing customer wagers made on previous rolls.

▶ Red chips represent payoffs made by the dealers.

▶ An "X" over a customer's wager signifies that it lost and the dealer collected it.

▶ An arrow indicates that a dealer has moved a customer's wager from one position to another.

▶ The dice number highlighted in the center of each layout is the number that affects all the wagers shown on that layout.

▶ A single circle represents a pile of chips and the number beside it equals the number of chips in the pile.

▶ A circle overlapping another circle is the symbol used when one pile of chips is placed on top of another pile. The fraction beside one of these symbols on the left-hand page identifies both the number of chips in the Odds Bet and the number of chips in the Come Bet. For example, the fraction $\frac{5}{3}$ means that 5 chips for the Odds Bet have been placed on top of, but slightly offset, the 3 chips for the Come Bet. See the diagram on top of page 58.

▶ When the symbol of a circle overlapping another circle is used on the right hand page, it represents an Odds Bet for either a Don't Pass or a Don't Come Bet. In this case, the fraction next to the symbol represents the Odds Bet only. For instance, the fraction $\frac{5}{1}$ means that 5 chips are leaning against a single chip, giving a total of 6 for the Odds Bet. (See the diagram at the right on top of page 59.) The fractions $\frac{2}{1}$ and $\frac{1}{1}$ give Odds Bet totals of 3 and 2.

For a newcomer to the game of Craps, it would be well to study carefully the next 29 layouts as they show the effects resulting from the throw of the dice on each successive roll. Since the Odds Bets are the only ones on which the player has no disadvantage, they are the most attractive bets to be wagered. The general explanations for Odds Bets are found on pages 46-55.

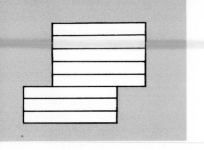

ODDS ON A
COME BET

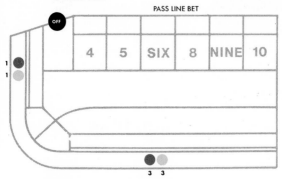

PASS LINE BET

| 4 | 5 | SIX | 8 | NINE | 10 |

PASS LI

PASS LI

| 4 | 5 | SIX | 8 | NINE | 10 |

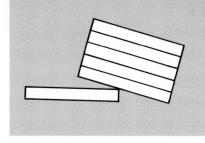

ODDS ON A DON'T COME
OR DON'T PASS BET

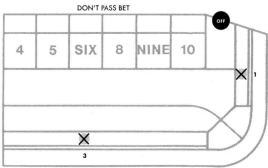

DON'T PASS BET

4	5	SIX	8	NINE	10

OFF

X 1

X
3

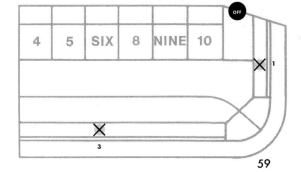

4	5	SIX	8	NINE	10

OFF

X 1

X
3

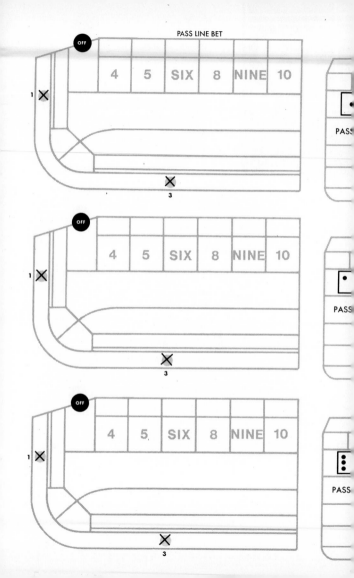

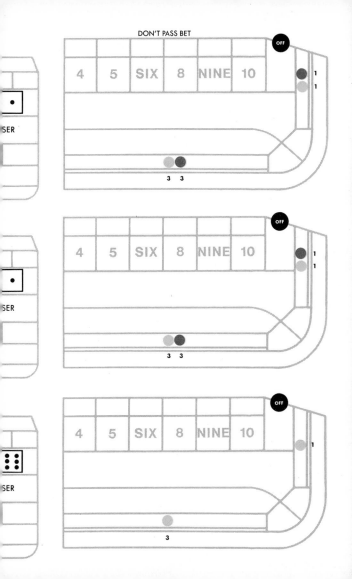

PASS LINE BET

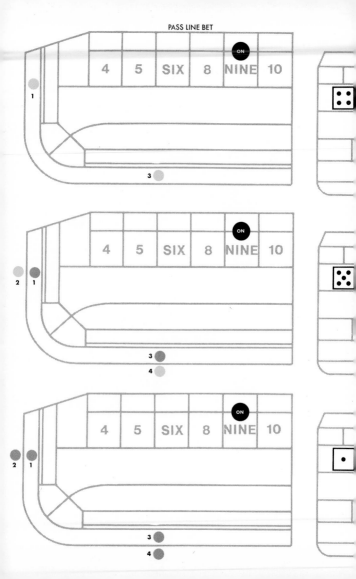

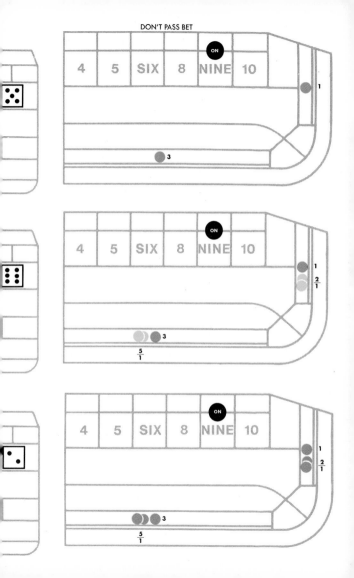

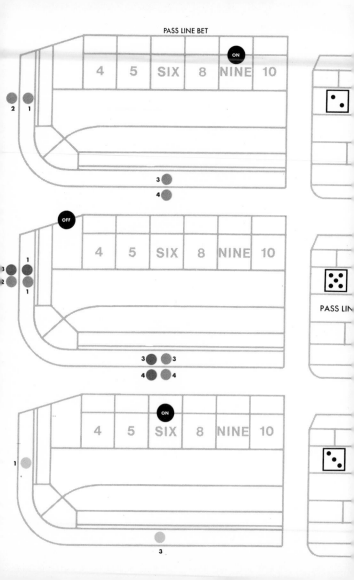

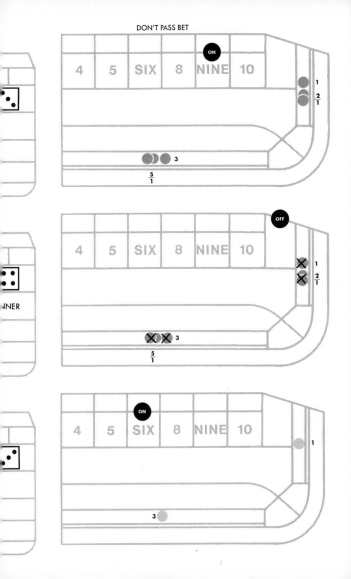

DON'T PASS BET

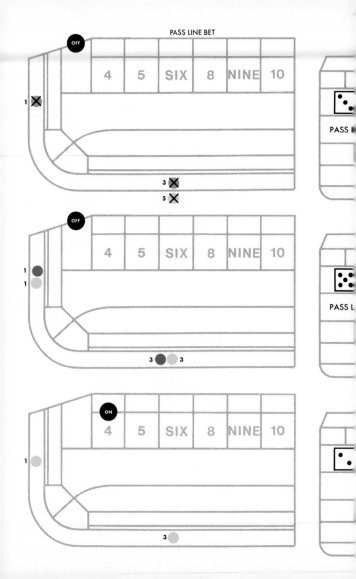

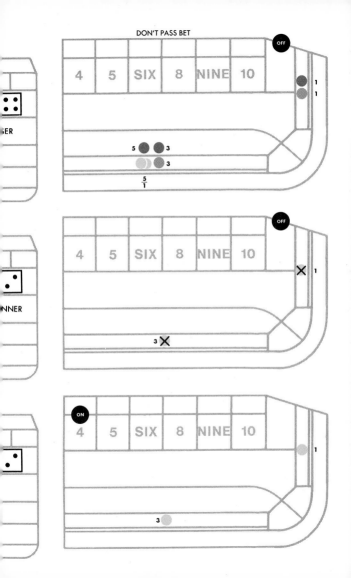

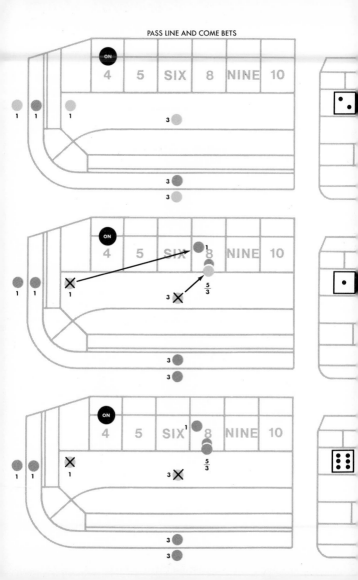

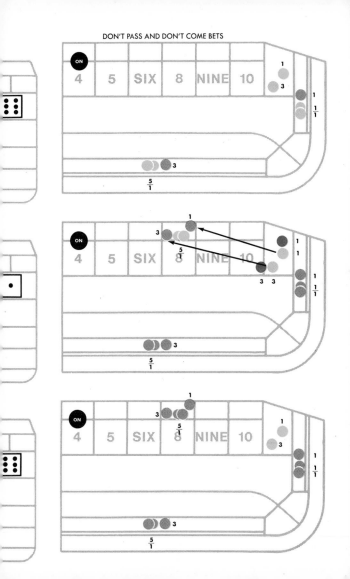

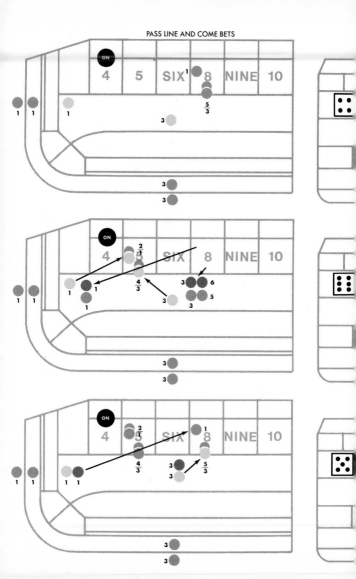

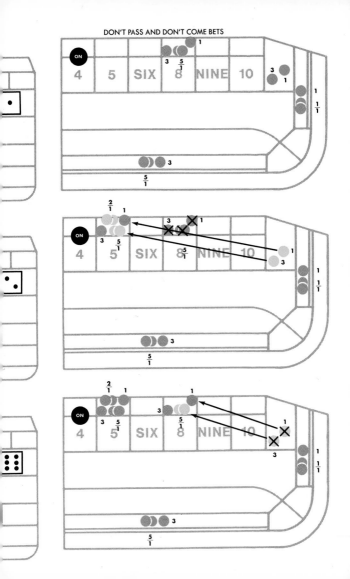

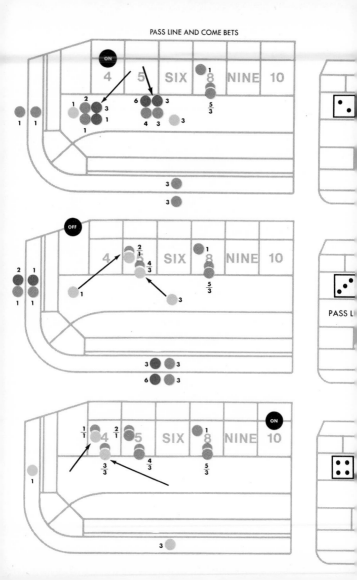

PASS LINE AND COME BETS

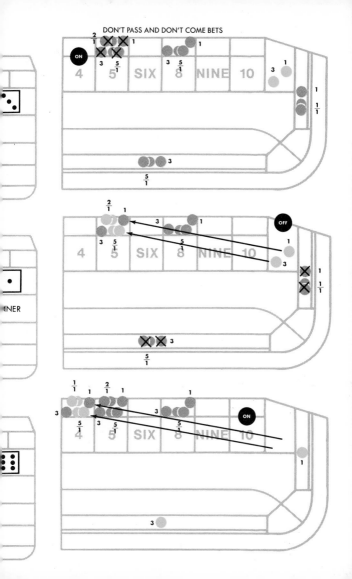

DON'T PASS AND DON'T COME BETS

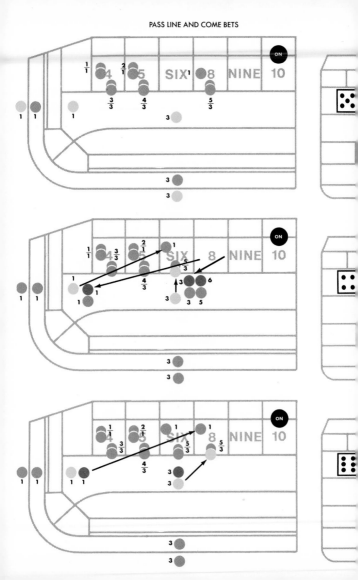

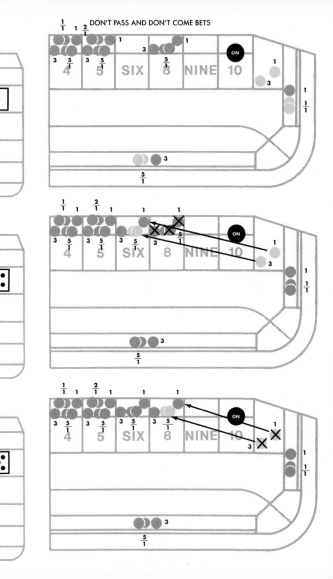

DON'T PASS AND DON'T COME BETS

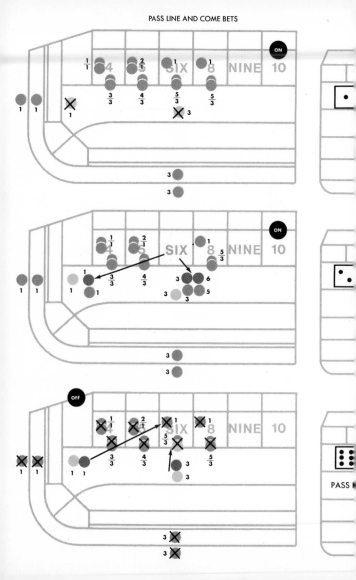

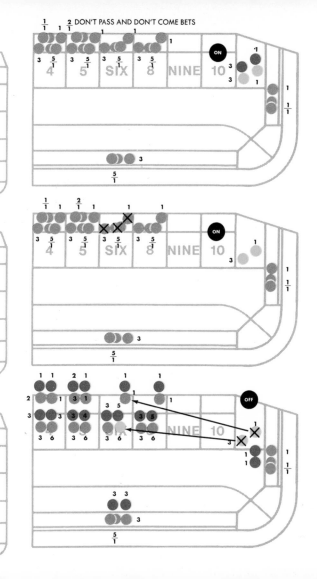

2 DON'T PASS AND DON'T COME BETS

CASINO ADVANTAGE

DO's		DON'Ts	
Pass	1.414%	Don't Pass	1.402%
Come	1.414%	Don't Come	1.402%
Place 6 or 8	1.515%	Lay 4 or 10	2.439%
Place 5 or 9	4.000%	Lay 5 or 9	3.225%
Place 4 or 10	6.667%	Lay 6 or 8	4.000%

PROPOSITIONS			
Field (20 to 19)	2.778%	Any Craps	11.111%
Field (20 to 18)	5.556%	3 or 11 (15 to 1)	11.111%
Big 6 or Big 8	9.091%	3 or 11 (14 to 1)	16.667%
Hard 6 or Hard 8	9.091%	2 or 12 (30 to 1)	13.889%
Hard 4 or Hard 10	11.111%	2 or 12 (29 to 1)	16.667%
	7	16.667%	

CRAPS BET PERCENTAGES are shown in the above chart listing the casino advantage for every Craps wager. The player is cautioned against taking the Craps wagers described in the rest of this chapter because these wagers have a higher casino advantage than the Pass, Come, Don't Pass and Don't Come wagers.

INDIVIDUAL POINT BETS, Buy, Place and Lay, are the three which let the player wager on the individual Point totals of his choice. The Buy and Place Bets win when the Point appears and lose on 7. The Lay Bet, the exact opposite, wins on 7 and loses when the Point appears. When the player wants to make a Buy, Lay or Place wager he sets his chips on the layout, usually in the Come box, and announces the bet to the dealer who sets the wager in the correct box or boxes.

4	5	SIX	8	NINE	10

THE PAYOFF CHIPS are placed directly in front of the player when Buy, Place and Lay wagers win. These chips should be removed from the layout immediately. These wagers are made in specific multiples. When a wager wins and the player wants to double the amount of his wager, he states "press" which instructs the dealer to double the amount of a winning Buy or Place wager before giving the remainder of the payoff to the player. These bets may be wagered or removed on any roll. The phrase "take down" instructs the dealer to remove these wagers which the dealer will set directly in front of the player.

The Buy and Place wagers, which are "Do" wagers because they win on the Point and lose on 7, are automatically "off" on Come-out rolls unless the dealer is informed that they are "working." When they work, the dealer sets either the Point marker or an "On" button on the player's wager. The Lay wagers, which are "Don't" wagers, always work when they are on the layout. When a player calls a Lay wager "down," even for one roll, the wager must be removed from the table. A description of each of these three Bets follows, but wagers should not be made because the player must wager more money than the table minimum (the best way to bet them requires 5 to 41 times the table minimum wager) against a relatively high casino advantage.

THE BUY BETS have the same payoff ratios as the Odds Bets. The Odds Bets have no casino advantage, but a "Commission" charge of 5% of the player's total wager creates the casino advantage for the Buy Bets. The smallest Commission charge is the table minimum.

The casino commission equals 5% because the wagers are made in multiples of 20 times the table minimum. For example, at a $1 minimum table, the wager would be $20. The $1 Commission is 5% of $20. Buy wagers are made in multiples of 21 times the table minimum, 20 units for the wager and 1 unit for the Commission. Therefore, the casino advantage is 4.762% and not 5% because the player loses an average of 1 unit for every 21 units he wagers.

Casinos will permit wagers of less than 20 units, but this increases the casino advantage, because the full Commission must be paid for each multiple of 20 units or partial multiple of less than 20 units. As an example, a $1 Commission on a $10 Buy wager increases the casino advantage from 4.762%

B

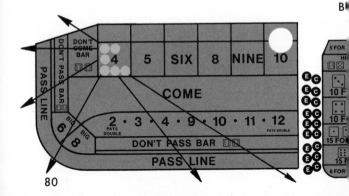

A SMALL "BUY" BUTTON is put on the wager to indicate it is to be paid according to the Odds ratios and not 1 to 1 as a Come wager would be. When the Point appears and the player wins, he must either take his original wager down with his winnings or pay the 5% Commission again for the next roll. If the player decides to remove his Buy wager before it wins or loses, the dealer also returns the Commission. Buy wagers are automatically off on Come-out rolls.

BUY BET PAYOFFS

Point	Payoff	Odds Ratio
4 or 10	40 to 20	2 to 1
5 or 9	30 to 20	3 to 2
6 or 8	24 to 20	6 to 5

to 9.09%. In contrast, some casinos will allow Buy wagers of $25 for a Commission of only $1. This reduces the casino advantage to 3.85%.

A player may Buy any single Point or any combination of Points on any roll. The player makes a Buy wager by setting his wager on the layout and calling out the Point he wants. The dealer removes the Commission for the casino as he puts the wager in the correct Point box. The wager is set in the Point box in the same way as a Come wager.

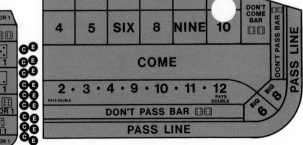

LAY BETS are the opposite of Buy Bets because they win on 7 and lose when the Point appears. Lay wagers are made in multiples of the pay-offs for the Buy wagers—24, 30 and 40 units.

Lay wagers win in multiples of 20 times the table minimum. The 5% Commission for Lay wagers is paid on the amount of the payoff; whereas, the 5% Commission for Buy wagers is paid on the amount of the wager. Thus, the Commission for both wagers is always paid on multiples of 20 units.

THE COMMISSION ON LAY WAGERS is paid on the amount of the payoff. For example, if the player Lays the Point 4 for $40 to win $20, he only pays a $1, not a $2 Commission. One dollar is only 2.5% of the $40 wager. The casino advantage for Lay wagers is less than the 4.762% for Buy wagers. The casino advantage for 4 and 10 is 2.44%, for 5 and 9, 3.23% and for 6 and 8 is 4.00%.

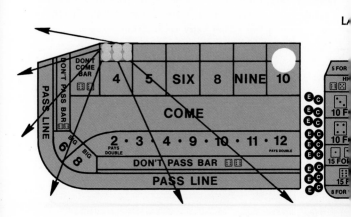

The player makes a Lay wager by setting his bet on the layout and calling out the Point or Points he wants. The dealer removes the Commission for the casino as he puts the wager in the correct Don't Point box. The dealer puts a small

LAY BET PAYOFFS		
Point	Payoff	Odds Ratio
4 or 10	20 to 40	1 to 2
5 or 9	20 to 30	2 to 3
6 or 8	20 to 24	5 to 6

"Buy" button on top of the wager to indicate it is to be paid according to the Odds ratios and not 1 to 1 as a Don't Come wager would be.

When 7 appears and the player wins, he must either take his original wager down with his winnings or pay the 5% Commission again for the next roll. If the player decides to remove his Lay wager before it wins or loses, the dealer also returns the Commission. Lay wagers work on every roll.

ET

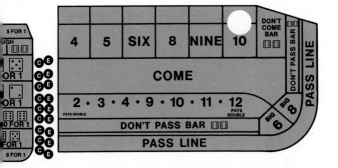

A PLACE WAGER can be made on any Point or any combination of Points on any roll. The player makes a Place wager by setting his bet on the layout and calling out the Points he wants. The dealer puts the wager on the line above or the line below the Come Point box in Las Vegas and in the Place Point box in Reno-Tahoe. In both cases, the wager is situated according to the player's location at the table. Place wagers can be removed on any roll, and they are automatically off on Come-out rolls.

Place Bets, depending on the Point, require wagers in multiples of 5 or 6 times the table minimum. They can be wagered for less, just like Buy Bets, but this increases the casino advantage.

PLACE POINTS, 6 and 8 have the least casino advantage of the Place Bets and are the best wagers to make next to the Do and Don't wagers—Pass and Come wagers. Points 4 and 10 have the highest casino advantage of the Place Bets and the 6.67% casino advantage is greater than the 4.76% for Buy Bets of the same Points. In terms of ca-

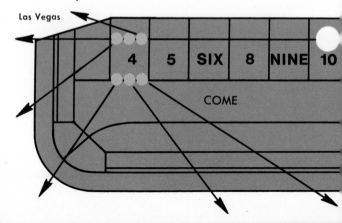

Las Vegas

PAYOFFS are based on the Odds ratios plus a 1 to 1 wager. The 1 to 1 wager of 1 unit creates the casino advantage because Place Bets do not win as often as they lose. For example, with Point 6 the Odds ratio is 6 to 5, so 1 unit is added to each side of the ratio to create a payoff of 7 to 6 units.

PLACE BET PAYOFFS

Point	Payoff	Odds Ratio
4 or 10	9 to 5	8 to 4
5 or 9	7 to 5	6 to 4
6 or 8	7 to 6	6 to 5

sino advantage, the Points 5, 6, 8 and 9 should be Placed rather than Bought, but 4 and 10 should be Bought if the player can afford the 21 unit minimum instead of the 5 unit minimum required to Place them. There are several popular ways of selecting the Points to be Placed, but none of them alter the casino advantage. The 2 "inside" Points, 6 and 8 are the best Place Bets. The 4 "inside" Points, 5, 6, 8 and 9 are also wagered together. "5 across" means all the Points except the one with the Point marker, and is wagered in multiples of 26 or 27 units, depending on the Pass Line Point. "6 across" means all 6 Points are Placed, and is wagered in multiples of

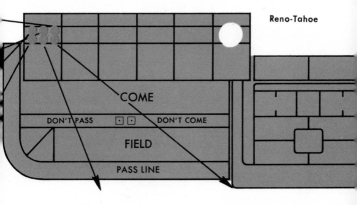

Reno-Tahoe

COME

DON'T PASS ⊡ ⊡ DON'T COME

FIELD

PASS LINE

32 units. Sometimes only the single Point opposite the Pass Line Point is bet. The opposite Points are 4 and 10 = 14, 5 and 9 = 14 and 6 and 8 = 14 because they are combinations on the opposite sides of the dice. The total on top of the dice and the total on the bottom of the dice always add up to 14.

PLACE vs. BUY BETS

	4	5	6	8	9	10
Place	6.67%	4.00%	1.52%	1.52%	4.00%	6.67%
Buy	4.76%	4.76%	4.76%	4.76%	4.76%	4.76%

BIG 6 AND BIG 8 wagers are set in position by the player. Each wins if the Point appears, in this example 6, and loses on 7. The dealer pays 1 to 1 next to the player's winning wager. Both the wager and the payoff remain for the next roll unless the player changes the amount or removes them altogether. Big 6 and Big 8 have the highest casino advantage, 9.091%, of all wagers in the outside sections of the layout. On the average, Big 6 and Big 8 lose 6

BIG 6 AND BIG 8 BETS

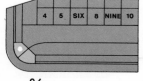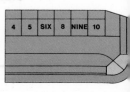

times faster than Placing 6 and 8, 1.52%, and twice as fast as Buying 6 and 8, 4.76%. For example, the player only wins 1 to 1 which is also 6 to 6, on the Big 6, but he wins 7 to 6 by Placing 6.

THE FIELD BET is also set in position by the player. This bet wins or loses on every roll. The player wins if any of the 7 totals printed in the Field appear, and the player loses if any of the other 4 totals, 5, 6, 7 or 8 appear.

In the field bet, the casino's 4 totals appear more often than the player's 7 totals so the Strip pays 1 to 1 if 3, 4, 9, 10 or 11 appear and 2 to 1 if 2 or 12 appear. The numbers that pay more than 1 to 1 are circled. The Downtown Las Vegas and Reno-Tahoe casinos increase the payoff on either 2 or 12 to 3 to 1 to reduce the Strip advantage of 5.56% to 2.78%. Although this is still a relatively high percentage, it makes this bet more desirable than the rest of the bets on the layout with the exception of the Pass Line, Come, Don't Pass, Don't Come, Place 6 and Place 8, and Lay 4 and Lay 10. Casinos in other areas of the world often have other payoff combinations and most of them increase the casino advantage. The dealer pays off next to the player's wager, and both stacks of chips remain for the next roll unless the player changes the amount.

FIELD BET

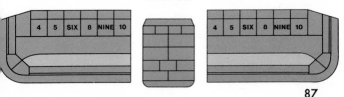

PROPOSITION BETS in the center of the layout, are handled by the stickman, who also controls the dice. A player makes a wager on a Proposition Bet by tossing his chips into the center of the layout as he announces the wager and the amount. For example, "Two dollar eleven." The stickman places the wager in the stated box unless the stickman is busy with the dice or other Proposition Bets. Then the stickman, boxman or dealer calls out the player's wager, which wins or loses on the next roll no matter where the chips lay.

PROPOSITION BETS

THE STICKMAN places the wager in the Proposition box according to the player's table location. If the wager wins, the stickman points out the winning player and announces the pay-off to the dealer who sets it in front of the player.

Proposition Bet payoffs do not include the amount of the play-

er's wager; his wager is left in the proposition box for the next roll. At any time, the player may direct the stickman to "take down" his wager and return it to him. Proposition Bets have a picture of the only winning dice combination and the amount of the pay-off listed in each box.

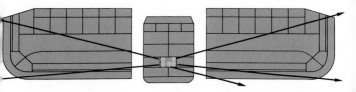

ONE-ROLL PROPOSTION BETS are wagered for only the next roll of the dice. They win if the dice combination pictured in the box appears, but they lose if any other combination appears.

Players generally make One-Roll wagers only on Come-out rolls because they contain the 5 totals which win (Natural 7 and 11) and lose (Craps 2, 3 and 12), but any one of these totals or any combination of them can be wagered at any time. It is interesting to note that when 7 appears, every wager on the layout either wins or loses so the table is cleared of wagers.

ONE ROLL BETS

5 FOR 1	SEVEN	5 FOR 1
HIGH		HIGH
10 FOR 1	8 FOR 1	
10 FOR 1	8 FOR 1	
15 FOR 1	30 FOR 1	30 FOR 1	15 FOR 1
15 FOR 1	15 FOR 1	
8 FOR 1	ANY CRAPS	8 FOR 1

89

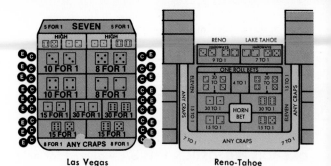

Las Vegas

Reno-Tahoe

"ANY CRAPS" is the three Crap numbers 2, 3 and 12. Any Craps wins if any of the three Crap totals 2, 3 or 12 appear. Eleven, Craps and the combination of Craps-Eleven are the most popular Proposition Bets. The stickman sets Craps-Eleven wagers either on the line which separates the two Bets or between the Craps and Eleven circles at the edge of the Proposition Bets that point to the player locations.

THE HORN BET is a combination of the Any Craps (2, 3 and 12) and 11. It must be wagered in multiples of 4 times the table minimum. It pays off according to the payoff for each individual total minus the 3 chips which were wagered on the other 3 totals which lost.

Horn High wagers are 5 unit wagers with 1 unit on each of 3 numbers and 2 units on the 4th. They pay off according to the individual totals. For 3 of the totals it would be the individual payoff minus the 4 losing chips, but for the 4th total it would be twice the individual payoff minus the 3 losing chips.

The Whirl wager of all 5 Come-out totals, 2, 3, 7, 11 and 12 is rarely made.

90

"TO" AND "FOR" are important words in gambling payoff ratios and it is important to distinguish between them. The word "To" indicates the player wins the payoff and also receives the amount of his original wager. The word "For" indicates the player wins only the payoff total. The player wins one unit less when "For" is used instead of "To."

PAYOFFS

TO	vs	FOR
Stated Payoff		Actual Amount
8 to 1		8 + 1 = 9
8 for 1		8 + 0 = 8

The payoffs for One-Roll wagers vary from casino to casino. Most downtown Las Vegas and Reno-Tahoe casinos pay one chip more for the totals 2, 3, 11 and 12 than the Strip casinos and this difference also affects Horn wagers because they are based on the four individual payoffs.

HOP BETS are One-Roll Bets that a single dice combination will appear on the next roll or "Hop" of the dice. The Reno-Tahoe layout, shown below, has a One-Roll wager for each of the four even numbered Points. Some casinos will let the player make a Hop wager for any single dice combination of his choice.

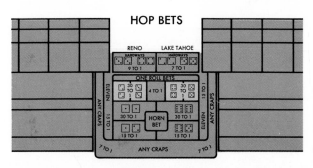

HOP BETS

HOP BET POSSIBILITIES

2	3	4	5	6	7	8	9	10	11	1
1 + 1	1 + 2	1 + 3 2 + 2	1 + 4 2 + 3	1 + 5 2 + 4 3 + 3	1 + 6 2 + 5 3 + 4	2 + 6 3 + 5 4 + 4	3 + 6 4 + 5	4 + 6 5 + 5	5 + 6	6 +

The player may wager that any of the possible dice combinations (shown above) will appear on the next roll or hop of the dice. A Hop wager loses unless the designated combination appears.

TO MAKE A HOP WAGER, the player tosses his chips to the boxman and calls out the dice combination. The boxman repeats the call as he sets the wager on the blank area of the layout directly in front of him. The Hop wagers are paid off according to the ratios for the printed One-Roll Bets which have the same probability of occurence and these payoff ratios vary from casino to casino. The 6 possible pairs are each paid off the same as a pair of 1's or 6's, and the 15 possible dice combinations made up of different numbers, for example, a 4 and 5, are each paid off the same as a 1 and 2 or 5 and 6. The 4 totals 5, 6, 8 and 9, no matter what combination creates the total, are paid off the same as Any Craps.

HARD vs. EASY COMBINATIONS		
Total	Hard Way	Easy Way
4	2 2	1 3
6	3 3	1 5 and 2 4
8	4 4	3 5 and 2 6
10	5 5	4 6

HARDWAY BETS

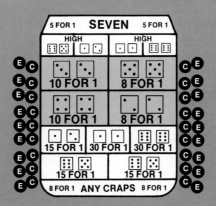

The Hard 6 and Hard 8 Bets pay 10 for 1 while the Hard 4 and Hard 10 Bets pay only 8 for 1, because there are more easy combinations that make the Hard 6 and Hard 8 lose.

HARDWAY PROPOSITIONS, are the 4 even numbered Point totals 4, 6, 8 and 10. They are usually made after a Point has been established to increase the amount wagered on the Point. "Hardway" means a pair of the same number and the player wins only if the Hard combination appears. For example, 2 and 2 for Hard 4. The player loses when either 7 or an "Easy" combination of the total appears. For example, 1 and 3 for Easy 4. The wager is not affected by any roll except when 7 or either the Hard or Easy combinations for the total appear. The Hardway Bets have a lower casino advantage than the other Proposition Bets but they still lose at a rate several times greater than the recommended wagers.

KENO

Keno uses the numbers 1 through 80 which are printed on tickets that are placed throughout the Keno lounge, or any other area that has been made available to players—dining rooms, bars, and casino. The players may select from one to fifteen of

A typical Keno counter is shown below.

these numbers on which to wager. Then the casino selects twenty of the eighty available numbers at random, and the amount the players win depends on the proportion of the players' choices that match those selected at random by the casino. The top payoff is $25,000 and it can be won in most casinos with a wager of only $1.20.

A standard unmarked Keno ticket is shown below.

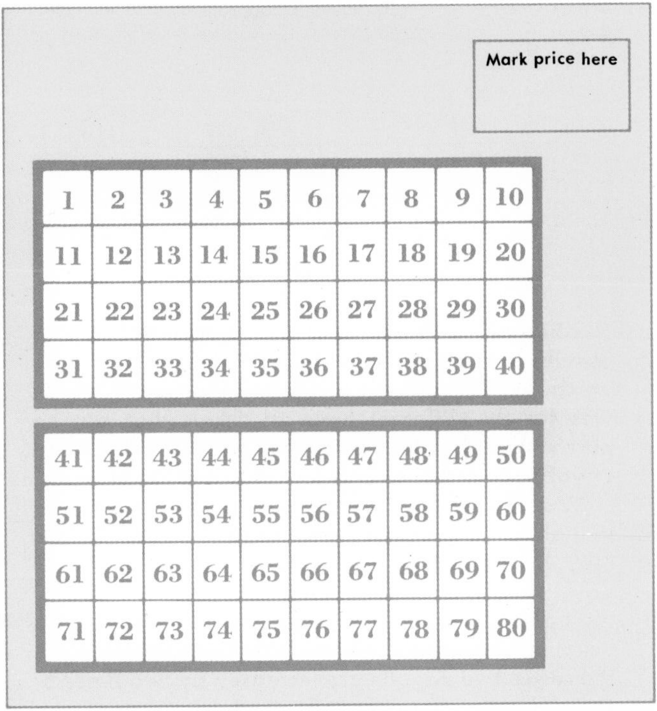

							Mark price here

1	2	3	4	5	6	7	8	9	10
11	12	13	14	15	16	17	18	19	20
21	22	23	24	25	26	27	28	29	30
31	32	33	34	35	36	37	38	39	40

41	42	43	44	45	46	47	48	49	50
51	52	53	54	55	56	57	58	59	60
61	62	63	64	65	66	67	68	69	70
71	72	73	74	75	76	77	78	79	80

PRICE
AND
PAYOFF SCHEDULE

MARK 4 SPOTS

Catch	Play 60¢	Play 1.20	Play 3.00
2 Pays	.60	1.20	3.00
3 Pays	2.50	5.00	12.50
4 Pays	70.00	140.00	350.00

MARK 8 SPOTS

Catch	Play 60¢	Play 1.20	Play 3.00
5 Pays	5.00	10.00	25.00
6 Pays	50.00	100.00	250.00
7 Pays	1,100.00	2,200.00	5,500.00
8 Pays	12,500.00	25,000.00	25,000.00

TICKET PRICES are contained in brochures that are usually located with the blank Keno tickets. These brochures list both the prices and the payoff schedules for the different types of tickets that can be purchased. The illustration shows the prices and payoffs for a 4-spot and for an 8-spot ticket.

Most tickets have a minimum wager of 60¢, although some casinos offer special rates. Tickets may be purchased in multiples of the minimum price and the payoffs are increased by similar multiples. For example, if the minimum price of a ticket is 60¢ and the player wagers $1.20 or $6.00, the respective payoffs are increased by two times or ten times the basic payoff schedule.

1	2	3	4	5	6	7	8	9	X
11	12	13	14	15	16	17	18	X	20
21	22	23	24	25	26	27	28	29	30
31	32	33	X	35	36	37	38	39	40

8

X	42	43	X	45	46	47	48	X	50
51	X	53	54	55	56	57	58	59	60
61	62	63	64	65	66	67	68	69	70
X	72	73	74	75	76	77	78	79	80

A COMPLETED KENO TICKET shows the player's choices and the price of the ticket. The player marks his choices with a black crayon (crayons are provided with the unmarked tickets) by placing an X over the numbers of his choice. He may select from one to fifteen of the eighty numbers. He then writes the number of choices he has made (in this example eight) on the right side of the ticket. He also writes the price of the ticket (the amount he is wagering) in the space designated for that purpose. Dollar signs and decimal points are never used. In the example shown, the price is 60¢ for the ticket. If the price is over $1.00, the cents are written over a line (1 $\underline{20}$, 6 $\underline{00}$; etc.).

KENO TICKETS ARE PURCHASED at the Keno windows located at the Keno counter, as shown in the photograph on page 94. The customer gives the ticket, or tickets, he has marked to a Keno writer along with the total purchase price. The Keno writer keeps the customer's original ticket and the amount of money for the purchase price. The writer makes a copy of the customer's ticket and gives the customer the duplicate copy. The writer also gives the customer any change that is due him.

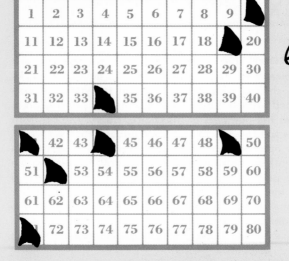

THE DUPLICATE COPY is identical to the original marked ticket with the exception that it has the game number printed on it. The customer can only win on the game having the number that appears on his copy, which is the next one that will be called. The customer should check to be sure that the duplicate copy is correct because it is his record of the spots he marked. The casino only pays off according to the numbers that were marked on the original ticket retained by the casino.

TWENTY WINNING NUMBERS are selected at random from a clear plastic bowl or a metal cage called a "goose." The goose contains eighty balls that are numbered from 1 through 80. All of the balls are mixed by an air current and twenty balls are blown, one at a time, into the two "rabbit ears" at the top of the goose. Some casinos have the goose rotate and a random ball is forced into the rabbit ears with each rotation. The caller announces over the Keno lounge public address system the number on each ball as it enters the rabbit ears.

The picture to the right shows ▶ Keno balls in the "goose" being blown up into the "rabbit ears." The numbers on these balls are lit up on the Keno board in the background.

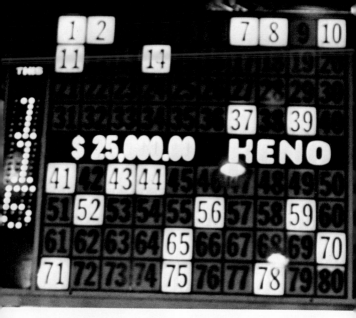

KENO BOARDS, usually located in the Keno lounge, the casino, and some of the areas for dining and drinking, light up the twenty numbers as they are called. The game number is also prominently displayed on the sign.

The twenty winning numbers are also punched into blank tickets that have the game number printed on them. These "draw" tickets are used by the employees and players to quickly determine winning tickets. When a "draw" ticket is placed over the player's original ticket or his duplicate copy, the marks on the winning numbers that were selected by the player show through the punched holes.

PAYOFF SCHEDULES for winning tickets are listed in the Keno brochures along with prices for the standard 1-spot to 15-spot tickets. There are variations in payoffs among casinos although there is general conformity among casinos in each locale.

PAYOFF SCHEDULE

MARK 4 SPOTS

Catch	Play 60¢	Play 1.20	Play 3.00
2 Pays	.60	1.20	3.00
3 Pays	2.50	5.00	12.50
4 Pays	70.00	140.00	350.00

MARK 8 SPOTS

Catch	Play 60¢	Play 1.20	Play 3.00
5 Pays	5.00	10.00	25.00
6 Pays	50.00	100.00	250.00
7 Pays	1,100.00	2,200.00	5,500.00
8 Pays	12,500.00	25,000.00	25,000.00

A 1-SPOT TICKET wins when the number the player selects is "caught" among the twenty winning numbers the casino draws. Except for some special tickets, all other tickets require more than one catch before they receive a payoff.

Once the necessary amount of spots is caught, each additional catch increases the size of the payoff. For example, the 60¢ 4-spot ticket schedule (shown above) requires at least two catches before it wins. The payoff increases when three or four numbers are caught. This 60¢ 8-spot ticket schedule requires a minimum of five catches to win, and the payoff increases as six, seven or all eight spots are caught.

101

WINNING TICKETS are paid by the Keno writers. When a customer presents his duplicate copy of a winning ticket at a Keno window, the writer verifies the amount of the payoff with his supervisor and then pays off the customer. The writer retains the customer's duplicate copy. A Federal regulation requires players to present winning tickets for payoff immediately after the game is called. The players always have several minutes before another game is called.

REPORTABLE KENO PAYOFFS

Price of Ticket	Reportable Payoffs
$ .00 to $ .59	$ 600. or over
.60 to .89	1,200. or over
.90 to 1.19	1,800. or over
1.20 to 1.79	2,400. or over
1.80 to 2.39	3,000. or over
2.40 to 2.99	3,600. or over
3.00 to 3.59	4,200. or over
3.60 to 9.99	6,000. or over
10.00 and over	10,000. or over

TAXES must be paid on winnings as indicated in the table. When a player wins a Keno payoff exceeding those in the table above, the casino will ask the player for his social security number and a piece of identification before it pays off. This information is sent to the Internal Revenue Service. Players are required to pay taxes on all gambling winnings unless they maintain acceptable records of their gambling losses. Income Tax Regulation Section 1.165-10 provides that gambling losses may be deducted from gambling winnings for income tax purposes, but gambling losses may not be deducted from income derived from any other source besides gambling.

REPLAYING TICKETS from earlier games is a convenience offered to players so they do not need to mark a new ticket when they play the same spots in the new game. The player turns in his duplicate ticket from a previous game with the purchase price to a Keno writer. The Keno writer treats this ticket as if it were the player's original and issues him a duplicate copy with the number of the next game printed on it.

KENO RUNNERS are available for the convenience of those players who desire to play Keno when they are not in the Keno lounge. A player may request any employee in the casino or in a dining or drinking facility to call a Keno runner. Keno runners carry blank tickets and black crayons. They take the players' original tickets and money to the Keno writers. The writers make duplicate copies of the players' tickets, and then the runners return the duplicate tickets and change to the players.

As soon as the game is called, the runner makes her rounds with a "draw" ticket to determine if the players have any winning tickets. The runner will take the players' duplicate copies of winning tickets to the Keno writers, collect the payoffs, and deliver the payoffs to the players.

If the Keno runner is late and does not get a player's ticket into the current game, the casino is not responsible. In this rare situation the player has the choice of having the runner either return his money or wager the ticket in the next game.

This pretty Keno runner is one of many serving the customers of the Stardust Hotel. ▶

A $25,000 PAYOFF is the biggest offered for a ticket. It is also the maximum payoff permitted for all the winning tickets in a given game. The State of Nevada prohibits a casino from paying out more than $25,000 in prize money in a single game. On those unusual occasions when the total payoffs for a game exceed $25,000, the casino pro-rates the payoffs so that each winning ticket receives a proportionate amount of the $25,000. For example, if there are two tickets in one game that win $25,000, and a third that wins $12,500, the first two would each receive $10,000 and the latter, $5,000.

THE CASINO ADVANTAGE for Keno is higher than for the other games. The casino advantage varies slightly for the different types of 1-spot to 15-spot tickets, but it approximates 25% for all of them. However, the game is very popular because it offers a big prize, $25,000 for a small wager, only $1.20, and it is also a slow and relaxing game so the casino advantage cannot be compared directly to the other games. In the other games, the casino takes a much smaller percentage per decision, but the games go so fast that its win-per-unit-of-time is higher than these percentage figures indicate because the percent advantage is always calculated on the basis of each decision rather than the length of time it takes to lose a given amount of money.

A COMBINATION TICKET can be written on a single ticket sheet if the spots are divided into separate groups. In the example on the next page, the twelve numbers that have been selected are divided into three groups of 4 spots. Three types of standard tickets can be wagered on this single Keno sheet. All spots within a circle must be wagered as a single unit. For instance, all of the spots in circle "A" must be wagered together. One, two or even three of the spots cannot be wagered independently of the others in the same group but the groups can be combined in different ways.

104

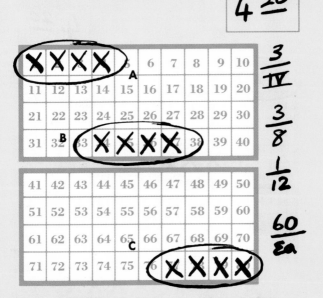

DIFFERENT COMBINATIONS are possible. In the above example, the smallest type of ticket that can be wagered is a standard 4-spot. All of the possible 4-spot tickets must be wagered at the same time because there is no way of indicating that some of the circles are being wagered and not the rest. If a player wants to create a 4-spot ticket, he has to wager on all three circles. This is a 3/4 (3 way 4-spot) ticket. Each circle is wagered as an independent standard 4-spot ticket, and each cir-cle is paid off according to the number of catches within it. The circles can be combined with each other, and the circles in the example can be combined into groups of two circles each to create 8-spot tickets. Three 8-spot tickets (A + B, A + C, and B + C) can be created in this example, and a player who wants to create 8-spot tickets must wager all three possible combinations at the same time as if they were three independent standard 8-spot tickets. This is a 3/8 (3 way 8-spot) ticket.

105

4 20

X	X	X	X	6	7	8	9	10
11	12	13	14	15	16	17	18	19	20
21	22	23	24	25	26	27	28	29	30
31	32	33	X	X	X	X	38	39	40

A

B

3/IV

3/8

41	42	43	44	45	46	47	48	49	50
51	52	53	54	55	56	57	58	59	60
61	62	63	64	65	66	67	68	69	70
71	72	73	74	75	76	X	X	X	X

C

1/12

60/Ea

This Keno ticket is repeated from the preceding page to make it easier for the reader to follow the text.

ALL THREE OF THE CIRCLES can be combined together (A + B + C) to create the single standard 12-spot ticket that existed before the circles were placed around the spots. This is a 1/12 (1 way 12-spot) ticket. Only three types of tickets can be wagered on this Keno sheet, a 3/4 ticket, a 3/8 ticket and a 1/12 ticket. A player has the right to wager any one of these three types of tickets, any two of them, or all three of them at the same time, and he writes his choices in the right hand margin of the sheet as well as the amount of his wager.

THE PLAYER'S CHOICES are called "conditions," and he only wagers on those types of tickets that he conditions. If the player conditions only one of the possible types of tickets, it is called a "way" ticket. If the player conditions more than one type of ticket, it is called a "combination" ticket. The illustration is a combination ticket because it has three types of tickets conditioned on it.

THE TOTAL PRICE of a ticket is based on the number of ways that have been conditioned on it because the player must wager each way that he conditions. In the example, the player is wagering the standard 60¢ minimum price for each conditioned way. The standard 12-spot (1 way 12-spot) ticket is 60¢. The 3/8 is three standard 60¢ 8-spot tickets that total $1.80. The 3/4 ticket is three standard 60¢ 4-spot tickets for another total of $1.80. The example has been conditioned seven ways:

	1 way	(12-spot)
	3 way	(8-spot)
+	3 way	(4-spot)

total 7 ways

The total price for the ticket is 7 ways times 60¢ which equals $4.20, and the total price, $4.20, is written in the upper right hand corner of the ticket. In the example, each type of ticket is wagered for 60¢ so the symbol "60 ea" (each way) or "60 W" (each way) is written in the lower right corner of the ticket. When all the conditioned tickets are not wagered for the same price, they are conditioned as the example on page 109. The price of each type of ticket is placed to the right of the symbol for each type of ticket, and a dash separates the ticket symbol and its price. The minimum price for a standard ticket is usually 60¢ but some casinos offer special "way-ticket" prices. Each way can be wagered for 30¢ or even less. Some casinos do not advertise their special "way" prices so the player should inquire what special prices are offered on "way" and "combination" tickets.

THE CASINO ADVANTAGE for way and combination tickets is the same as for standard tickets. Wagering on several standard tickets at the same time increases the player's probability of winning, but it proportionately increases his purchase price. The purpose of way and combination tickets is to save the players and writers time in marking tickets between games. However, they do create interesting variations with multiple winning possibilities on a single Keno sheet.

CORRECT CONDITIONING is required on way and combination tickets or players will not be paid the complete payoff on winning tickets. A player's conditions must not permit more than one interpretation. Otherwise, the casino will be forced to pro-rate the payoff according to the total number of ways that the player should have wagered the ticket based on the player's own conditions. The problem of an incorrectly conditioned ticket rarely occurs because the Keno writers carefully examine way and combination tickets for accuracy before they accept wagers from the players. The player can avoid needless errors by using the following rules to condition his way and combination tickets. When the circles on way and combination tickets all contain the same number of spots, the player should calculate the total number of ways the circles can be combined to create a specific type of ticket.

The ticket in the example has 8 circles, each with 3 spots. There are 5 different "way tickets" that can be conditioned on it:

8 way   3-spot ticket (the individual circles)
28 way   6-spot ticket (groups using 2 circles)
56 way   9-spot ticket (groups using 3 circles)
70 way 12-spot ticket (groups using 4 circles)
56 way 15-spot ticket (groups using 5 circles)

Tickets cannot be created with more than 15 spots; therefore, groups of six, seven or all eight of the circles, each with 3 spots, cannot be combined together in this example because these groupings would produce tickets with 18, 21 and 24 spots respectively. The player can select any one or any combination of the five different types of way tickets above and write the proper conditions in the

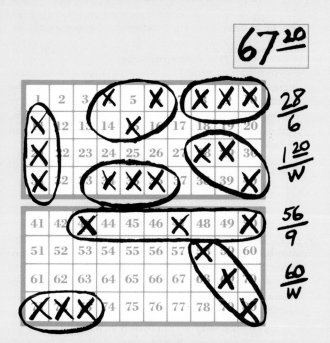

right hand margin, but once the player has chosen which type of tickets he will wager, he must calculate the total number of ways each type of ticket can be wagered. In the example above, the player has selected 6-spot tickets and 9-spot tickets. The formula that follows is used to calculate the number of ways each one of these tickets can be created with 8 circles, each with 3 spots.

1) A fraction is created. The term "numerator" refers to the numerals on the top of the fraction, and

the term "denominator" refers to the numerals below the line, i.e., $\frac{\text{numerator}}{\text{denominator}}$. The denominator always begins with the numeral 1 on the left and increases in sequence, i.e., $1 \times 2 \times 3 \times 4$, etc. The number of numerals in the denominator is equal to the number of circles (never the number of spots) that are being combined to increase the specific type of ticket.

28 way 6-spot (using 2 circles)

$$\frac{}{1 \times 2} =$$

56 way 9-spot (using 3 circles)

$$\frac{}{1 \times 2 \times 3} =$$

2) The numerator always begins with the total number of circles (never the number of spots) that have been drawn on the ticket and decreases in sequence, i.e., $8 \times 7 \times 6 \times 5$, etc. The number of numerals in the numerator is always equal to the number of numerals in the denominator.

28 way 6-spot (using 2 circles)

$$\frac{8 \times 7}{1 \times 2} =$$

56 way 9-spot (using 3 circles)

$$\frac{8 \times 7 \times 6}{1 \times 2 \times 3} =$$

3) The numerator and denominator are canceled and then multiplied out.

28 way 6-spot (using 2 circles)

$$\frac{4 \times 7}{1 \times 1} = 28$$

56 way 9-spot (using 3 circles)

$$\frac{4 \times 7 \times 2}{1 \times 1 \times 1} = 56$$

4) The result is the total number of ways that the circles can be combined to produce the specific type of ticket. The number of ways for each type of ticket are conditioned in the right corner: 28/6 (28 way 6-spot) and 56/9 (56 way 9-spot).

5) The price for each type of ticket is multiplied by the number of ways that the ticket can be created: $1.20 × 28 ways = $33.60 and $.60 × 56 = $33.60. Then the prices for each conditioned ticket are added together to obtain the total price for the ticket: $33.60 + $33.60 = $67.20.

In the example, p. 112 , some circles contain 5 spots, others contain 4 spots, and the remaining circles contain 3 spots. When the circles on "way" and "combination" tickets contain different numbers of spots, the following formula is used to calculate the total number of ways the circles can be combined to create the specific type of ticket. The formula is simple. All of the circles that contain a certain number of spots are multiplied by all of the circles that contain another number of spots.

For example, 8-spot tickets can be created by combining each 3-spot circle with each 5-spot circle. Three circles contains 5 spots and 4 circles contain 3 spots so 3 × 4 = 12 ways. There is one other way of creating an 8-spot ticket in this example. The two circles that contain 4 spots combine to create a single 8-spot ticket, which makes a total of 13 ways of creating an 8-spot ticket in this illustration. The customer must wager every possible way there is of creating the type of ticket he conditions; in this case he must wager all 13 ways.

Groups of 4 or less spots should be enclosed within circles, and groups of 5 or more spots should

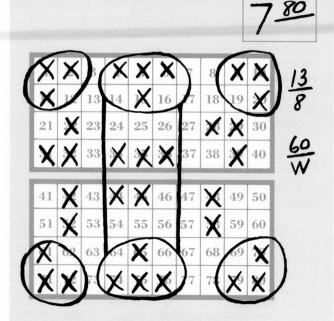

be enclosed within lines, as this ticket illustrates. However, there are situations in which groups of 5 or more numbers must be circled for clarity.

A WAY TICKET PAYOFF is calculated after the number of catches in each circle is determined. Keno writers mark the catches with long slashes as shown in the ticket on p. 113. This is a "way" ticket because there is only one condition in the right hand margin. If it were a combination ticket with more than one condition, each type of condition would be evaluated individually using the following method for "way" tickets, and the payoffs for each condition would be added together to obtain the total payoff.

The easiest and most accurate method to calculate the payoff for a "way" ticket is shown in the table on p. 114. First, a fraction is created. The number of numerals that appear in both the numerator and the denominator is equal to the number of circles. The numerals in the numerator represent the number of spots in each circle, for example, 3 spots in each of 5 circles. The numerals in the denominator represent the number of catches in each circle.

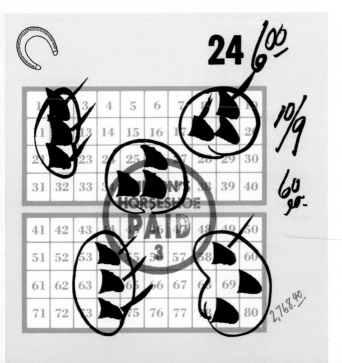

A step-by-step analysis is made of every possible payoff. It begins with the largest number of catches and continues down to the least number of catches. The only reason that the 2-1-0 catch is included (3 catches on a standard 9-spot ticket does not win any payoff) is to list every possible combination. The total number of combinations of catches is always equal to the total number of ways that have been conditioned. In this example there are 10 conditioned ways and 10 combinations of catches. When the customer calculates every combination of catches, he ensures that he will not miss any combination that might win a payoff.

$$\frac{\text{(Circles) } 3\text{-}3\text{-}3\text{-}3\text{-}3}{\text{(Catches) } 3\text{-}3\text{-}2\text{-}1\text{-}0} = 10 \text{ way 9-spot}$$

1)	3-3-2	1/8	$2,500.00
2)	3-3-1	1/7	180.00
3)	3-3-0	1/6	28.00
4)	3-2-1	1/6	28.00
5)	3-2-1	1/6	28.00
6)	3-2-0	1/5	2.00
7)	3-2-0	1/5	2.00
8)	3-1-0	1/4	.20
9)	3-1-0	1/4	.20
10)	2-1-0	1/3	+ .00
	TOTAL PAYOFF	=	**$2,768.40**

HIGH LOW TICKETS are special "way" tickets that casinos list in their Keno brochures because they have unique payoff schedules. Most casinos offer a 12-spot High Low Ticket payoff as shown on the opposite page. The 12 spots are divided into 3 circles, each having 4 spots, and the ticket is conditioned "HL" in the right hand margin to differentiate the High Low Ticket from the standard 4-spot and standard 12-spot tickets and payoff schedules. The 12-spot High Low Ticket and the standard 12-spot have different payoffs for each number of catches, but these differences are balanced statistically so the casino advantage is approximately the same for both. One ticket pays more for a lot of catches, while the other ticket pays more for a few catches.

HIGH LOW TICKET, 12 SPOTS

3 Groups of 4

Play	Rate 60¢	Rate 90¢	Rate 1.80
2-2-1	.30	.50	1.00
3-1-1	.40	.60	1.20
3-2-0	.45	.70	1.40
4-1-0	.60	.90	1.80
2-2-2	2.80	4.20	8.40
3-2-1	3.30	5.00	10.00
4-1-1	4.40	6.60	13.20
3-3-0	4.40	6.60	13.20
4-2-0	4.90	7.40	14.80
3-2-2	17.65	26.50	53.00
3-3-1	21.40	32.10	64.20
4-2-1	25.10	37.70	75.40
4-3-0	32.60	48.90	97.80
3-3-2	91.30	137.00	274.00
4-2-2	118.65	178.00	356.00
4-3-1	146.00	219.00	438.00
4-4-0	228.00	342.00	684.00
3-3-3	375.00	562.50	1,125.00
4-3-2	440.00	660.00	1,320.00
4-4-1	570.00	855.00	1,710.00
4-3-3	1,240.00	1,860.00	3,720.00
4-4-2	1,704.40	2,556.65	5,113.30
4-4-3	4,083.30	6,124.95	12,249.90
4-4-4	12,500.00	18,750.00	25,000.00

A KENO-style ticket figure with handwritten markings.

Top right box: 1 $\frac{20}{}$

First grid (numbers 1–40):

1	2	3	4	5	6	7	X	9	10
11	12	13	14	15	16	X	18	19	20
21	22	23	X	X	26	27	28	29	30
X	32	33	34	35	36	37	38	⊗	40

Right margin: $\frac{1}{8}$ $\frac{1}{9}$

Second grid (numbers 41–80):

41	42	43	44	45	46	47	48	49	50
X	52	53	54	55	56	X	58	59	60
61	62	63	64	65	66	67	68	X	70
71	72	73	74	75	76	77	78	79	80

Right margin: $\frac{60}{\text{Ea}}$

A KING TICKET is one having circles that contain only 1 spot. A King circle is treated just like any other circle, but it is given special acknowledgment because any standard ticket can be converted easily into a combination ticket by simply circling only 1 spot. In the example above, the standard 9-spot ticket also is a standard 8-spot ticket.

In the unusual example above right, all 5 spots are circled as King spots. Each circle can be com-

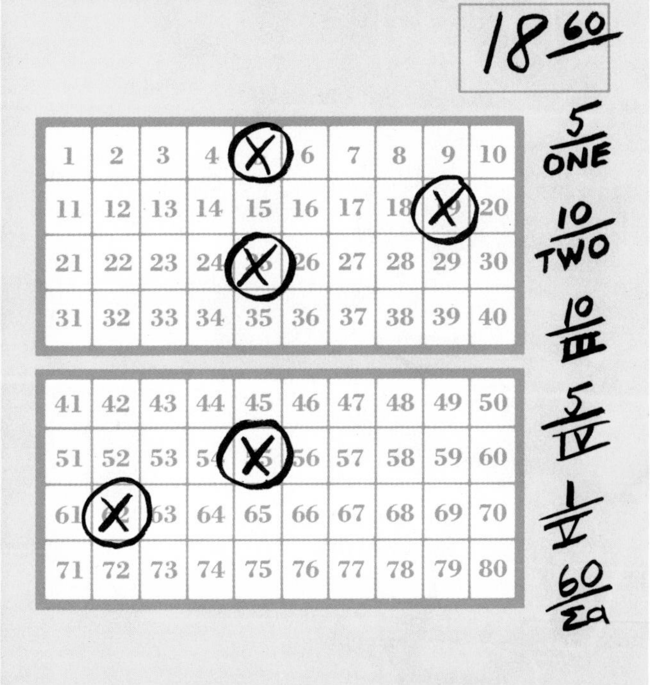

18 60

5/ONE

10/TWO

10/III

5/IV

1/V

60/Σa

bined with every other circle to create 1-spot through 5-spot tickets. Every possible combination in this example has been conditioned. This illustration contains the symbols used by most casinos to condition 1-spot through 5-spot tickets. The words "one" and "two" are written out for 1-spot and 2-spot tickets. Roman numerals are used to denote 3-spot, 4-spot, and 5-spot tickets and Arabic numerals are used to identify 6-spot to 15-spot tickets.

117

BACCARAT
(pronounced Bäh-cah-rah)

Baccarat games are usually partitioned off by a rail
from the rest of the gaming area. This affords the
players a degree of privacy because they often have
large sums of money exposed on the table. Two
hands are dealt in the game of Baccarat, and every
player has the option of wagering on either hand.
Two or three cards are dealt to each hand, and the
hand with the point total closest to 9 wins.

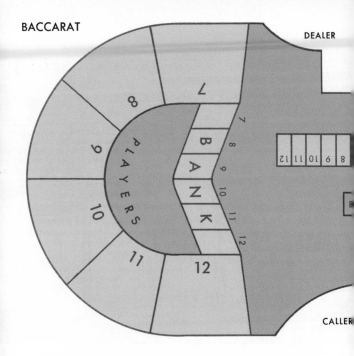

SEAT NUMBERS are placed in the spaces in front of every chair in order to identify each player's hands and wagers. The seats are numbered 1 through 12. If there are more than 12 seats, the numbers continue with 14. The number 13 is generally eliminated to accommodate any superstitious beliefs on the parts of those players who consider the number 13 to be an unlucky number. The Bank Hand Bet boxes and the Commission Marker boxes are numbered to correspond with the seat numbers.

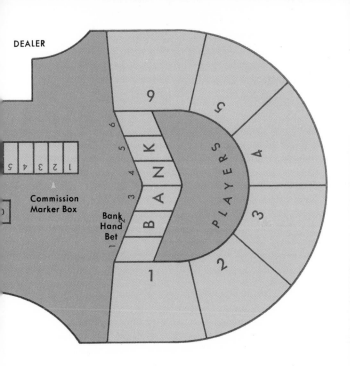

THREE EMPLOYEES operate each Baccarat game. The two dealers in the center of the table are responsible for the wagers on their respective sides of the table. They collect losing wagers and pay winning wagers. They also record, in the row of Commission Marker boxes in front of them, the commission money each player owes the casino. On the opposite side of the table, the caller directs the game. The caller tells the players when to deal, and he announces the winning hand.

TWO HANDS of cards are dealt in each game of Baccarat—the "Bank Hand" and the "Player Hand." These names are arbitrary, and they mean no more or less than "Hand Number 1" and "Hand Number 2." The player has the option of wagering on either hand, and he may switch from one hand to the other on successive deals.

BANK HAND WAGERS are placed in the numbered boxes labeled "bank" that are highlighted in the

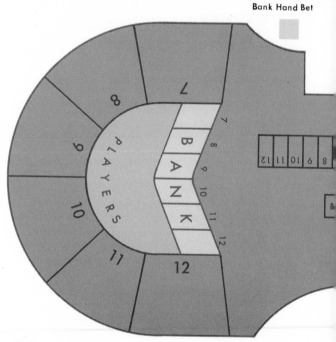

Bank Hand Bet

illustration below. Each player uses the Bank Hand box that contains his seat number.

PLAYER HAND WAGERS are placed in the areas that are highlighted in the illustration below. Many casinos do not divide the Player Hand Bet areas into individual boxes. In these casinos each player sets his wager just across the line from his seat space in the Player Hand area with his money pointing towards himself.

Player Hand Bet

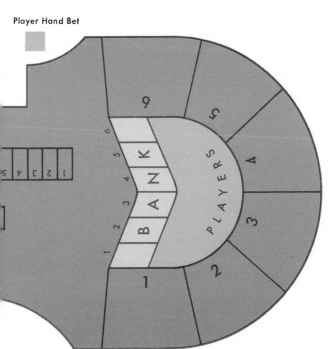

CARD VALUES—Tens and picture cards—jacks, queens and kings—equal 0. Aces equal 1. The rest of the cards count their face value. The four suits, spades, hearts, diamonds and clubs, have no meaning in Baccarat.

HAND VALUES

Only numerals in red count

$$\boxed{2} + \boxed{3} = \boxed{5} \qquad \boxed{2} + \boxed{1} + \boxed{4} = \boxed{7}$$

$$\boxed{0} + \boxed{9} = \boxed{9} \qquad \boxed{0} + \boxed{3} + \boxed{7} = \boxed{10}$$

$$\boxed{8} + \boxed{9} = \boxed{17} \qquad \boxed{8} + \boxed{3} + \boxed{5} = \boxed{16}$$

HAND VALUES—When the two or three cards in a single hand are added together, only the right hand number of the final figure counts. It is the point total for the hand. For example, $8 + 9 = 17$. Only the 7 counts so the hand equals 7. The only possible point totals are 0 to 9 (0, 1, 2, 3, 4, 5, 6, 7, 8 and 9), and the hand with the point total closest to 9 wins.

THE DEALERS SHUFFLE together the eight standard 52 card-decks used to play the game of Baccarat, and some casinos permit the players to assist with the shuffle.

A joker or a card with a different colored back is inserted near the end of the combined decks, and then these decks are placed in a dealing box called a "shoe."

CARD VALUES

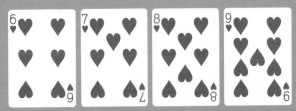

Each card = Face value

Each card = 0

Ace = 1

THE BURN CARDS—The caller removes the first card from the shoe, and he turns it face up. The point value of this card (in this case, picture cards are worth ten points) specifies the number of cards that are to be "burned." The appropriate number of burn cards are removed from the shoe and discarded into the bowl in the center of the table. In the illustration below, the first card removed from the shoe is a 3, so three more cards are burned before the first hand is dealt to the players.

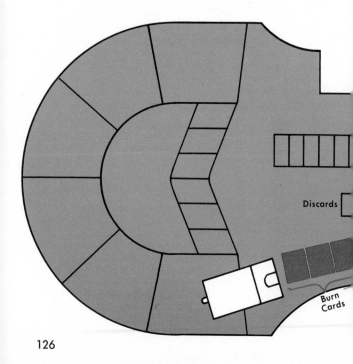

CARDS FROM COMPLETED HANDS are placed in the discard bowl by the caller. When the shuffled cards are almost depleted, the joker appears in the front of the shoe. At that point, the hand in progress is completed, and the caller halts the deal. Before a new deal begins, all the decks are shuffled together again. The casino has the option to reshuffle the cards after the completion of any hand, even if the joker has not yet appeared; but the casino is not supposed to reshuffle if a hand is in progress.

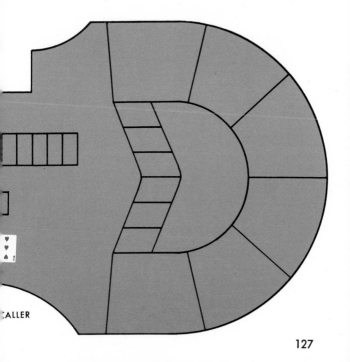

CALLER

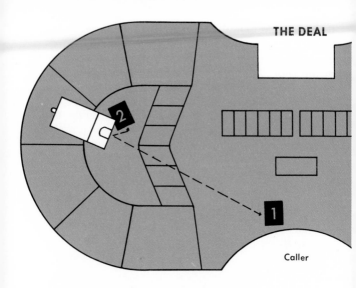

Caller

THE RIGHT TO DEAL is optional. If a player does not want to deal, he does not have to. When he is given the shoe, he merely passes it to the player on his right, but most players like to hold the shoe and deal. The player must wager at least the table minimum on either the Bank Hand Bet or the Player Hand Bet before he may deal the cards, and the player may switch his wager from one bet to the other after each hand is completed. The player may continue to deal hands as long as the Bank Hand continues to win, but as soon as the Player Hand Bet wins, the player must pass the shoe and the right to deal to the player on his right. The shoe always travels in a counterclockwise motion.

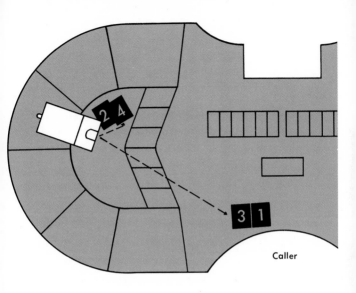

Caller

THE CALLER SUPERVISES THE DEAL by the player who has the shoe after every player has wagered on either the Bank Hand Bet or the Player Hand Bet. The caller's instruction, "cards", directs the player to deal two cards, face down, to each hand.

The player slides the first card, which is for the Player Hand, to the caller.

The player tucks the second card, which is for the Bank Hand, under the front corner of the shoe that is farthest away from the caller so that it will not be in the way when the remaining cards are dealt. The player slides the third card to the caller. The player tucks the fourth card under the previous Bank Hand card.

129

THE HANDS ARE FACED, turned face up, after they are dealt. The caller gives the two Player Hand cards, which are face down, to a player who has a wager on the Player Hand Bet, and the caller usually gives the cards to the player with the biggest Player Hand wager. This player immediately turns the cards face up, and he then tosses them back to the caller. The caller announces the point total for the two cards, and he lays them down in front of him in the Player Hand card area. When none of

FACING

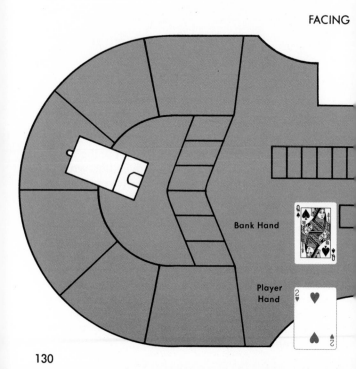

Bank Hand

Player Hand

the players make a Player Hand wager, the caller faces the Player Hand cards himself and sets them down in the Player Hand area.

After the Player Hand cards are set down, the player who dealt removes the two Bank Hand cards from under the corner of the shoe. He faces the cards, and then tosses them to the caller. The caller announces the point total for the two cards, and he lays them down in front of him in the Bank Hand card area.

HE HANDS

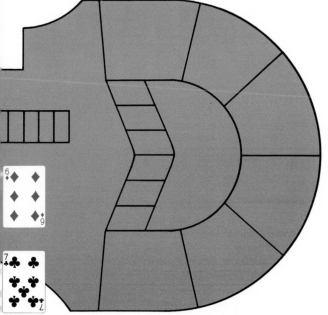

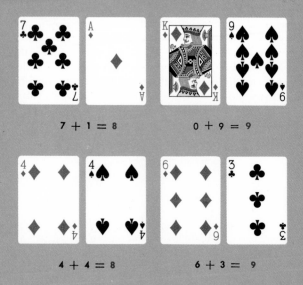

$7 + 1 = 8$ $0 + 9 = 9$

$4 + 4 = 8$ $6 + 3 = 9$

Only numerals in red count

A NATURAL HAND is made up of two cards that total 8 or 9. When either the Bank Hand or the Player Hand is dealt a Natural 8 or 9, neither hand may draw a third card. The hand is now complete so the caller faces the cards and immediately declares the hand with the highest point total the winner. Natural 9 wins over all other point totals including Natural 8.

132

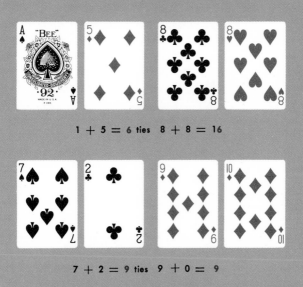

1 + 5 = 6 ties 8 + 8 = 16

7 + 2 = 9 ties 9 + 0 = 9

A TIE HAND occurs when both the Bank Hand and the Player Hand have the same point total at the conclusion of the deal. A tie hand is often referred to as a "push", "draw" or "standoff," and when the two hands tie, none of the wagers win or lose. The original wagers again belong to the players, and the players have the choice of wagering again on either hand or quitting.

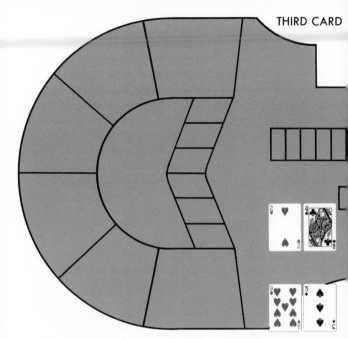

"Bank wins, 7 over 3."

THE THIRD CARD is the final card that can be dealt to either hand. The third card rules are mandatory. They dictate in every situation whether a third card must be dealt or cannot be dealt to either hand. Most players deal without knowing the third card rules because the caller directs their deal according to these fixed rules. The player with the shoe never deals a third card until the caller requests it, and then the player always deals a third card face up to the caller who lays it next to the initial two cards as he announces the new point total for the hand.

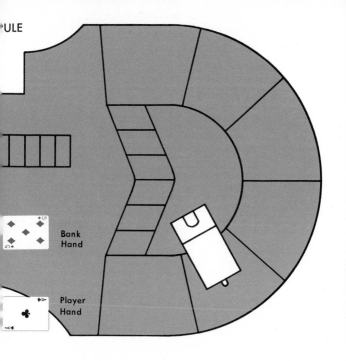

When the third card rules require the Player Hand to stand on the initial two cards, the caller states, "Player stands with (point total)." When the rules require a third card for the Player Hand, the caller requests a "card for the Player." After the Player Hand is concluded, the Bank Hand is completed in the same fashion. When both hands are complete, the caller declares the hand with the highest point total the winner. For example, "Bank wins, 7 over 3," or "Player wins, 1 over 0," or in the case of a tie, "Tie hand, 6 to 6, nobody wins."

THE PLAYER HAND MUST STAND IF THE POINT TOTAL OF THE INITIAL TWO CARDS IS 6 OR MORE (6, 7, 8 OR 9), AND THE PLAYER HAND MUST DRAW A THIRD CARD IF THE POINT TOTAL OF THE INITIAL TWO CARDS IS 5 OR LESS (1, 2, 3, 4 OR 5).

WHEN THE PLAYER HAND STANDS because it has a point total of 6 or 7 on the initial two cards, the third card rules for the Bank Hand are identical to the Player Hand third card rules stated at the top of this page. Thus, when the Player Hand stands with 6 or 7, the Bank Hand must also stand with a point total of 6 or 7 on the initial two cards, but the Bank Hand must draw a third card if it has a point total of 5 or less.

WHEN THE PLAYER HAND DRAWS a third card because it has a point total of 5 or less on the initial two cards, the third card rules for the Bank Hand, when the Bank Hand has a point total of 3 to 6 (3, 4, 5 or 6) on the initial two cards, are different from the Player Hand third card rules. The third card rules that govern the Bank Hand are determined by the point value of the third card drawn by the Player Hand.

THE BANK HAND MUST STAND IF THE POINT TOTAL OF THE INITIAL TWO CARDS IS 7 OR MORE (7, 8 OR 9), AND THE BANK HAND MUST DRAW IF THE POINT TOTAL OF THE INITIAL TWO CARDS IS 2 OR LESS (0, 1 OR 2).

THIRD CARD RULES
WHEN BANK HAND TOTALS 3 to 6

Bank Hand Total	Bank Hand DRAWS if Player Hand Drew		Bank Hand STANDS if Player Hand Drew	
3	1-2-3-4-5-6-7	9-10	8	
4	2-3-4-5-6-7		1	8-9-10
5	4-5-6-7		1-2-3	8-9-10
6	6-7		1-2-3-4-5	8-9-10

WHEN THE BANK HAND POINT TOTAL is 3 to 6 on the initial two cards and the Player Hand has drawn a third card, the point value of the third card drawn by the Player Hand is the factor that determines whether the Bank Hand stands or draws. These Bank Hand third card rules are presented in the diagram above. The two sections of the diagram, "Bank Hand Draws" and "Bank Hand Stands," are exact opposites. They are opposite because the point value of the third card drawn by the Player Hand requires that the Bank Hand draw a third card in the left hand section and stand on the initial two cards in the right hand section of the diagram.

These third card rules create a unique gaming situation. Even when the initial two card point total for the Bank Hand is

greater than the three card point total for the Player Hand, the Bank Hand may still be forced to draw a third card, which may reduce its point total. The decision to draw a third card in these situations is solely determined by the point value of the third card drawn by the Player Hand, not the needs of the Bank Hand. For example, if the Bank Hand has a point total of 4 on its initial two cards and if the Player Hand has a point total of only 3 after drawing a 2 for its third card, the Bank Hand still must draw a third card.

The Bank Hand must draw a third card because the Player Hand drew a 2 for its third card. In this example, the Bank Hand will reduce its point total and lose if it draws a 6, 7 or 8, and it will tie if it draws a 9 as its third card.

MINIMUM AND MAXIMUM WAGERING LIMITS are higher for the game of Baccarat than the other casino games. The most typical minimum wagering limit is $20 although there are some $5 minimum games. The usual maximum wagering limit is $2,000.

Casinos pay off in cash at the Baccarat tables. Each player lays his money in the numbered space directly in front of his chair. The players wager with $20 and $100 bills, and $5 bills are used when the minimum wagering limit is $5. $500 chips are available for large wagers. Players may exchange the casino chips they obtain at the other games for currency at the Baccarat tables.

WINNING PLAYER HAND PAYOFFS are always in the ratio of one to one. For example, a $5 payoff for every $5 wager, a $20 payoff for every $20 wager, etc. The casino has an advantage because the Player Hand loses more often than it wins. It loses more often than it wins because of the differences in the third card rules for the Player Hand and the Bank Hand.

WINNING BANK HAND PAYOFFS are also in the ratio of one to one. Since the Bank Hand wins more often than it loses, the casino creates an advantage by charging a 5% commission on all winning Bank Hand payoffs. The dealers pay off $5 for every $5 wager, $20 for every $20 wager, etc., but each time

138

a player wins a Bank Hand wager he owes the casino 5% of the payoff. In reality the player wins only $19 for every $20 he wagers on the Bank Hand. However, the dealers pay off one to one, $20 to $20, and tally up the commission charges separately because it simplifies each payoff and speeds up the game.

COMMISSION MARKERS are used to record the commission obligations of each player. Every time a dealer pays off a winning Bank Hand wager at the ratio of one to one, he places a commission marker equal to 5% of the payoff, 25¢ on a $5 payoff, $1 on a $20 payoff, $5 on a $100 payoff, etc., in the commission marker box containing the player's seat number. Each time a player wins a Bank Hand wager, 5% of the payoff is added to the total amount in the commission marker box that contains his seat number.

Players owe the amount of their commission markers to the casino upon demand. The dealers usually request the players to pay their commission obligation every time the combined decks of cards are shuffled, and players must pay their commission markers before they leave the table.

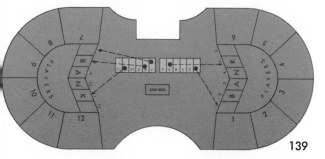

THE CASINO ADVANTAGE for the Bank Hand Bet and the Player Hand Bet are approximately the same. The casino advantage occurs with the Player Hand Bet because the player loses more often than he wins. The casino advantage occurs with the Bank Hand Bet, even though the player wins more often than he loses, because the casino only pays off 95¢ for every $1 wagered, when the 5% commission is deducted from the payoff.

The Bank Hand has a slightly lower casino advantage than the Player Hand, because even with the 5% commission, the Bank Hand wins often enough to make it a better bet than the Player Hand. There is a great deal of disagreement among mathematicians as to the exact casino advantage on these two bets. The author's mathematical approximation of the casino advantage indicates that Richard A. Epstein probably has the correct figures in his book "The Theory of Gambling and Statistical Logic" (page 215). He lists the Bank Hand casino advantage at 1.16% and the Player Hand casino advantage at 1.37%. These two bets have the lowest casino advantage except for the Odds Bets in the game of Craps when they are added to the Pass, Come, Don't Pass and Don't Come Bets.

PROPOSITION BETS are occasionally added to Baccarat layouts, but none of them has become standardized at the time of this printing. The Proposition Bets, as those in the game of craps, have always had a high casino advantage. The player should wager only on the Bank Hand Bet, and possibly the Player Hand Bet, unless he thoroughly understands a Proposition Bet and its casino advantage.

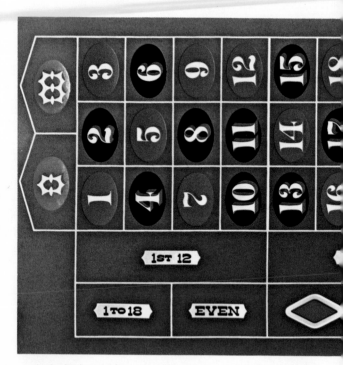

At the Roulette table, a player may wager on 1, 2, 3, 4, 5, 6, 12, or 18 numbers at one time. If the player's wager is on the same number

THE ROULETTE TABLE in Nevada has a wheel with thirty-eight numbered metal pockets in which the rotating ball may land and a layout which has the same thirty-eight corresponding numbers. Eighteen of the numbers, 1 to 36, are red and eighteen are black. Zero and 00 are both green.

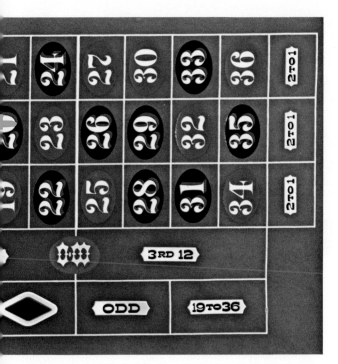

as the one on which the ball lands on the Roulette wheel, the player wins; otherwise, his wager loses.

The player should be careful that each chip fits clearly on the bet he desires because every bet wins or loses on each spin of the ball. If a player cannot reach a certain bet, he can slide his wager toward the dealer and tell him which number or combination of numbers to place it on.

THE PLAYER may wager with currency, regular casino chips, or Roulette chips. Roulette chips have no monetary value printed on them and can be purchased from the dealer at the table with either currency or regular casino chips.

The player receives a set of distinctly colored Roulette chips which no one else may use. Roulette chips are used because there is only one place on the Roulette layout to make each bet. When more than one player makes the same bet, the chips are piled on top of one another, so the owners of winning chips are identified by the colors.

When the player purchases Roulette chips he declares their value, which may be any amount between the table minimum and table maximum, and

the dealer places a coin or a numbered marker button on the set of colored chips to indicate their value. Instead, he may place the marker on top a colored chip on the rim of the wheel. If the value of the chip is the table minimum, some casinos do not use a marker.

ROULETTE CHIPS are purchased in quantities of twenty, called "stacks." Before leaving the table, the player must cash in his Roulette chips for regular chips because the Roulette chips have no value printed on them and cannot be used or exchanged anywhere in the casino except at the table where they were purchased.

COST OF CHIPS

Stack of chips		Chip value		Purchase price
20 chips	×	$ .10	=	$ 2.00
20 chips	×	$ .25	=	$ 5.00
20 chips	×	$ .50	=	$10.00
20 chips	×	$1.00	=	$20.00

ON THE INSIDE of the layout the player may wager from 1 to 6 numbers by placing his chips directly on the numbers and the lower borderline.

ON THE OUTSIDE of the layout the player may wager on 12 or 18 numbers by placing his chips in the twelve large betting boxes.

INSIDE

	00	3	6	9	12	15	18	21	24	27	30	33	36	2 to 1
		2	5	8	11	14	17	20	23	26	29	32	35	2 to 1
	0	1	4	7	10	13	16	19	22	25	28	31	34	2 to 1

1st 12	2nd 12	3rd 12
1 to 18	EVEN	RED	BLACK	ODD	19 to 36

OUTSIDE

1 NUMBER BET PAYS 35 TO 1

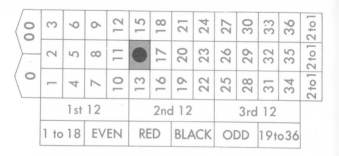

	00	3	6	9	12	15	18	21	24	27	30	33	36	2 to 1
		2	5	8	11	●	17	20	23	26	29	32	35	2 to 1
	0	1	4	7	10	13	16	19	22	25	28	31	34	2 to 1

1st 12	2nd 12	3rd 12
1 to 18	EVEN	RED	BLACK	ODD	19to36

WHEN A CHIP IS CENTERED on the single winning number, the player is paid 35 to 1. Each wager wins on the next spin if the wager covers the number on which the ball lands; otherwise it loses. Each of the thirty-six red and black numbers and green 0 and 00 may be wagered individually. Zero and 00 are treated exactly like the other numbers: they win and lose in the same way and pay the same odds.

38 WAYS TO BET 1 NUMBER
2 INVOLVE 0 AND 00

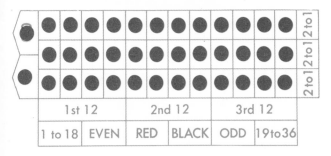

	1st 12		2nd 12		3rd 12	
1 to 18	EVEN	RED	BLACK	ODD	19 to 36	

A 2 NUMBER BET may be wagered by placing a chip across any line that separates two numbers. If the ball lands on either number, the bet pays 17 to 1.

2 NUMBER BET PAYS 17 TO 1

00	3	6	9	12	15	18	21	24	27	30	33	36	2 to 1
	2	5	8	11			20	23	26	29	32	35	2 to 1
0	1	4	7	10	13	16	19	22	25	28	31	34	2 to 1

1st 12			2nd 12			3rd 12		
1 to 18	EVEN		RED	BLACK		ODD	19to36	

THERE IS ONLY ONE BET that may be made at two different locations on the layout. The split bet between 0 and 00 may be made on the line that separates the two green numbers or on the line that separates the 2nd Dozen and 3rd Dozen bets on the outside of the layout. Most casinos do not have the bet printed on the outside of the layout, but it is accepted in all casinos for the convenience of the players.

63 WAYS TO BET 2 NUMBERS
6 INVOLVE 0 AND 00

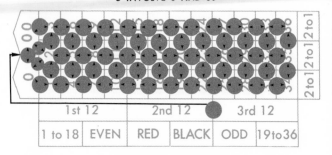

3 NUMBER BET PAYS 11 TO 1

00	3	6	9	12	15	18	21	24	27	30	33	36	2 to 1
	2	5	8	11	14	17	20	23	26	29	32	35	2 to 1
0	1	4	7	10	13	16	19	22	25	28	31	34	2 to 1

1st 12		2nd 12		3rd 12	
1 to 18	EVEN	RED	BLACK	ODD	19 to 36

15 WAYS TO BET 3 NUMBERS
3 INVOLVE 0 AND 00

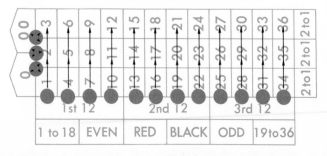

4 NUMBER BET PAYS 8 TO 1

00	3	6	9	12	15	18	21	24	27	30	33	36	2 to 1
	2	5	8	11	14	17	20	23	26	29	32	35	2 to 1
0	1	4	7	10	13	16	19	22	25	28	31	34	2 to 1

1st 12	2nd 12	3rd 12

1 to 18	EVEN	RED	BLACK	ODD	19 to 36

22 WAYS TO BET 4 NUMBERS

00	3	6	9	12	15	18	21	24	27	30	33	36	2 to 1
	2	5	8	11	14	17	20	23	26	29	32	35	2 to 1
0	1	4	7	10	13	16	19	22	25	28	31	34	2 to 1

1st 12	2nd 12	3rd 12

1 to 18	EVEN	RED	BLACK	ODD	19 to 36

THE ONLY FIVE NUMBER BET on the layout contains the numbers 0, 00, 1, 2 and 3. The Player should avoid this bet because his disadvantage is 50% greater than for the other bets. On this bet, the player will lose an average of 3 out of every 38 chips wagered; whereas, on every other bet, the player will lose an average of only 2 out of every 38 chips wagered.

5 NUMBER BET
PAYS 6 TO 1

00	3	6	9	12	15	18	21	24	27	30	33	36	2 to 1
0	2	5	8	11	14	17	20	23	26	29	32	35	2 to 1
	1	4	7	10	13	16	19	22	25	28	31	34	2 to 1

1st 12			2nd 12			3rd 12		
1 to 18	EVEN	RED	BLACK	ODD	19 to 36

6 NUMBER BET
PAYS 5 TO 1

00	3	6	9	12	15	18	21	24	27	30	33	36	2 to 1
0	2	5	8	11	14	17	20	23	26	29	32	35	2 to 1
	1	4	7	10	13	16	19	22	25	28	31	34	2 to 1

1st 12			2nd 12			3rd 12		
1 to 18	EVEN	RED	BLACK	ODD	19 to 36

11 WAYS TO BET 6 NUMBERS

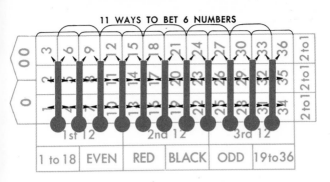

6 WAYS TO BET 12 NUMBERS
PAYS 2 TO 1

00													2 to 1	2 to 1
	3	6	9	12	15	18	21	24	27	30	33	36		
	2	5	8	11	14	17	20	23	26	29	32	35		2 to 1
0	1	4	7	10	13	16	19	22	25	28	31	34		
	1st 12				2nd 12				3rd 12					
	1 to 18	EVEN		RED		BLACK		ODD		19to36				

12 NUMBER COLUMN BET
PAYS 2 TO 1

00													2 to 1
	3	6	9	12	15	18	21	24	27	30	33	36	
	2	5	8	11	14	17	20	23	26	29	32	35	
0	1	4	7	10	13	16	19	22	25	28	31	34	2 to 1
	1st 12				2nd 12				3rd 12				
	1 to 18	EVEN		RED		BLACK		ODD		19to36			

12 NUMBER DOZEN BET
PAYS 2 TO 1

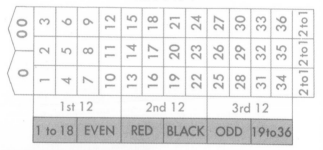

0 00	3	6	9	12	15	18	21	24	27	30	33	36	2 to 1
	2	5	8	11	14	17	20	23	26	29	32	35	2 to 1
	1	4	7	10	13	16	19	22	25	28	31	34	2 to 1
	1st 12				2nd 12				3rd 12				
	1 to 18		EVEN		RED		BLACK		ODD		19 to 36		

6 WAYS TO BET 18 NUMBERS
PAYS 1 TO 1

0 00	3	6	9	12	15	18	21	24	27	30	33	36	2 to 1
	2	5	8	11	14	17	20	23	26	29	32	35	2 to 1
	1	4	7	10	13	16	19	22	25	28	31	34	2 to 1
	1st 12				2nd 12				3rd 12				
	1 to 18		EVEN		RED		BLACK		ODD		19 to 36		

THE LOW NUMBERS of 1 through 18 or the high numbers of 19 through 36 may be wagered, and if the ball lands on one of the winning numbers, the player is paid 1 to 1.

THE EVEN NUMBERS (those divisable by 2) or the odd numbers may be wagered. Both bets lose, just as all Outside Bets do, when the ball lands on either green 0 or 00.

18 NUMBER HIGH AND LOW BETS
EACH PAYS 1 TO 1

00	3	6	9	12	15	18	21	24	27	30	33	36	2 to 1
	2	5	8	11	14	17	20	23	26	29	32	35	2 to 1
0	1	4	7	10	13	16	19	22	25	28	31	34	2 to 1

1st 12				2nd 12				3rd 12			
1 ● 18		EVEN		RED		BLACK		ODD		19 ● 36	

18 NUMBER EVEN AND ODD BETS
EACH PAYS 1 TO 1

00	3	6	9	12	15	18	21	24	27	30	33	36	2 to 1
	2	5	8	11	14	17	20	23	26	29	32	35	2 to 1
0	1	4	7	10	13	16	19	22	25	28	31	34	2 to 1

1st 12				2nd 12				3rd 12			
1 to 18		E●N		RED		BLACK		O●D		19 to 36	

18 NUMBER RED AND BLACK BETS
EACH PAYS 1 TO 1

00	3	6	9	12	15	18	21	24	27	30	33	36	2 to 1
	2	5	8	11	14	17	20	23	26	29	32	35	2 to 1
0	1	4	7	10	13	16	19	22	25	28	31	34	2 to 1

1st 12				2nd 12				3rd 12			
1 to 18		EVEN		R●D		BL●CK		ODD		19 to 36	

PAYOFFS are made when the ball comes to rest in one of the pockets. The dealer announces the number while pointing to it on the layout. Then the dealer sweeps in all of the losing wagers before paying off the winning wagers.

First the dealer pays off the Outside wagers individually in the bet spaces, and then the dealer calculates the total payoff for the winning Inside wagers and slides it across the table to directly in front of the player. All winning wagers and the pay-offs on the Outside Bets remain on the layout for the next spin of the ball unless the player removes all or any part of them.

As soon as the dealer has paid off all the winning wagers, the player may start wagering for the next spin of the ball, and he may continue wagering until the dealer calls "No more bets," as he hears the ball hit the metal pockets. Any bets made after this time are simply returned to the player whether he wins or not.

PAYOFFS

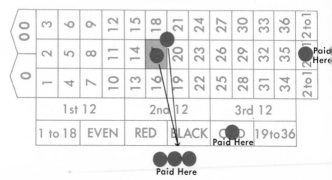

Paid Here

Paid Here

Paid Here

154

Dealer pointing to winning number

ROULETTE TABLES have both a chip minimum and a table minimum. The table minimum depends on the chip minimum. A 10¢ chip minimum has a table minimum of 50¢ or less, and a 25¢ chip minimum has a table minimum of $1. Each Outside Bet the player wagers requires at least the table minimum, and the maximum for each Outside Bet is usually $250 or $500.

OUTSIDE BETS

0 0	3	6	9	12	15	18	21	24	27	30	33	36	2 to 1
	2	5	8	11	14	17	20	23	26	29	32	35	2 to 1
0	1	4	7	10	13	16	19	22	25	28	31	34	2 to 1

1st 12			2nd 12			3rd 12		
1 to 18	EVEN	RED	BLACK	ODD	19 to 36

THE INSIDE BETS also require at least the table minimum, but several different bets may be made with smaller value chips which total that amount. For example, when the table minimum is \$1, four 25¢ chips may be placed on any combination of Inside Bets. Always ask the dealer what the table and chip minimums are. The maximum on any single Inside Bet is usually \$25 or less.

THE HOUSE ADVANTAGE for all bets, except the single five number bet, is 5.26% because the casino will win an average of 2 chips for every 38 wagered. For example, if the player wagers 1 chip on number 14 every spin, in a cycle of 38 spins he will lose on 37 numbers and win 35 chips when number 14 appears. He would win only 35 chips while losing 37, and the casino would be ahead 2 chips.

The house advantage is the same for the other bets which involve more numbers because the bets pay off correspondingly smaller amounts of chips. For example, if the player wagers on a split between the two numbers 14 and 17, he will lose on

36 numbers and win 17 two times when numbers 14 and 17 appear. The player would win only 34 chips while losing 36, and the casino would again be ahead 2 chips.

The same results can be worked out for every bet except the single five number bet. In this case the player will lose on 33 numbers and win 6 chips five times when the numbers 0, 00, 1, 2 and 3 appear. He would win only 30 chips while losing 33, and the casino would be ahead 3 chips. The casino wins 50% faster on this bet than any of the others, and the house advantage is 7.89%.

EUROPEAN ROULETTE is played in most casinos throughout the world. It also has 36 red and black numbers and green 0, but it does not have Nevada Roulette's green 00 so a five number bet combination is not possible. The payoffs are the same in both games, but the house advantage in European Roulette is only 2.70% compared to 5.26% in Nevada Roulette because the player loses an average of 1 chip for every 37 wagered instead of 2 chips for every 38 wagered.

6 EN PRISON BETS

0	00												
	3	6	9	12	15	18	21	24	27	30	33	36	2 to 1
	2	5	8	11	14	17	20	23	26	29	32	35	2 to 1
	1	4	7	10	13	16	19	22	25	28	31	34	2 to 1

1st 12			2nd 12			3rd 12		
1 to 18	EVEN		RED	BLACK		ODD	19 to 36	

WHEN THE "EN PRISON" BET is offered in European Roulette, the house advantage is reduced to only 1.35% because the player only loses one half of his wager when 0 appears. In a variation of the En Prison Bet, the player does not lose any of his wager when 0 appears because the dealer places the entire wager on the line which borders the bet. The decision is made on the next spin, but in this case the player only wins back his initial wager which is equivalent to wagering one half of it again.

HOUSE ADVANTAGE			
NEVADA ROULETTE 0 and 00		**EUROPEAN ROULETTE** 0 only	
Five Number Bet	All Other Bets	En Prison Bets	All Other Bets
7.89%	5.26%	1.35%	2.70%
Lose 3 of 38 Chips Bet	Lose 2 of 38 Chips Bet	Lose 1 of 74 Chips Bet	Lose 1 of 37 Chips Bet

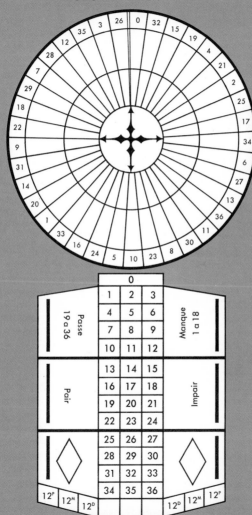

MORE INFORMATION

NOTE: Among the many books that have been published on games and gambling, the following are the ones that are listed as the best sellers by the Gambler's Book Club* in Las Vegas, Nevada, and are the ones recommended by the author of this guide.

Goodman, Mike, HOW TO WIN, Holloway House Publishing Company, All America Distributors' Corp., Los Angeles, 1971.

Jacoby, Oswald, OSWALD JACOBY ON GAMBLING, Hart Publishing Company, New York 10003, 1963.

Lemmel, Maurice, GAMBLING NEVADA STYLE, Dolphin Books, Doubleday & Company, Inc., New York 10017, 1966.

Noir, Jacques, CASINO HOLIDAY, Oxford Street Press, Berkeley, California 94709, 1970.

Revere, Lawrence, PLAYING BLACKJACK AS A BUSINESS, Lyle Stuart, Inc., New York 10003, 1973.

Silberstang, Edwin, PLAYBOY'S BOOK OF GAMES, Playboy Press, Chicago, Illinois 60611, 1972.

Thorp, Edward O., BEAT THE DEALER, Vintage Books, Random House, New York 10022, 1966.

Wilson, Allan N., CASINO GAMBLER'S GUIDE, Harper & Row, Publishers, New York 10016, 1970.

Wykes, Alan, COMPLETE ILLUSTRATED GUIDE TO GAMBLING, Doubleday & Company, Inc., New York 10017, 1964.

*A catalogue of publications (more than 500 titles on gambling) will be mailed upon request by the Gambler's Book Club, P.O. Box 4115, Las Vegas, Nevada 89106.

A B C D E